Stories for Harry

by

Rosemary Westwell

To the best of my knowledge, the text for 'The Man from Snowy River' is in the public domain but if you know differently, please contact me immediately.

The text here is reproduced from the Gutenberg Project:
http://www.gutenberg.org/files/213/213-0.txt accessed 13/03/2018

PARENTAL GUIDANCE is advised.

Prologue

When my grandchild, Harry, was seven years old he said:
'Nanna, will you tell me some stories from the olden days?'

Well, Harry, here they are. My facts may not be absolutely correct for the memory can play tricks on you at times, but these stories are very true to the way I felt at the time.
I hope you enjoy them.
love
Nanna Roe

Chapter one

When I was a baby

The year was 1947. I was a little baby lying down in my pram watching and listening to the new sights and sounds that surrounded me. I had just been fed and all was well with the world. I was in Tasmania, Australia, a warm country, a little warmer than England and I felt cosy and contented, even when the clear blue sky began to change colour and there was a little chill in the air. Dusk was falling and my tiny eyes followed the heavy pinks and different shades of mauve in the sky. The varied movements of the tree fascinated me.

My mum and dad were inside our house in Ashgrove Street – the back end of Devonport, Mum used to say. Every night, after feeding and putting my brother Peter and I to bed, my parents liked to settle down at the kitchen table to have a few beers and tell stories, laughing and joking a lot so that Dad could relax after a hard day at work. Mum cooked their meal on a big black fuel stove in the kitchen. She banged the saucepans a lot as she filled them with water and put them on the plate on top of the stove to boil. She joined Dad at the kitchen table while it came to the boil.. Then she quickly peeled some potatoes and carrots, washed some silver beet from the garden and put them in the saucepans to cook while searing the steaks on another plate. She hated housework, or anything that took her away for having a good time with her friends, so she did everything as fast as she could – going at things like a bull at a gate, she used to say.

Mum and Dad lingered over their meal, still talking and laughing until it was time to go to bed. They may have had a few too many beers, but they didn't worry, for they had time to sleep them off overnight – at last Dad was relaxed and able to have a peaceful night's sleep. It was only a couple of years after the end of the war – a worrying time when Dad had been away overseas for years, fighting the enemy: the Germans led by Hitler in places like Egypt, Palestine, New Guinea and Greece.

That night Mum and Dad did the usual chores, washing-up in the sink, stoking up the fire in the stove with large chunks of wood so that it wouldn't not go out overnight and hanging up the washing on the handles of the oven doors to dry. Mum quickly ironed a shirt for Dad with the iron that had been heated up on the stove. They went to their bedroom and as they were changing into their pyjamas, Dad had a niggling thought. He was sure there was something that they had forgotten. Suddenly he slapped his hand on his head. 'The baby!' he cried. They had forgotten to bring me in from outside and put me to bed!

How do I know this? Dad told this story to all my friends when I got married in England many, many years later.

Chapter two

Kindergarten

The kindergarten was in Best Street, high up on the top of the hill in Devonport, Tasmania. It was a long low building of white weatherboard that shone brightly in the sun. My mum took me to the front entrance and I thought we were just visiting. Mum talked for some time to the tall lady at the door and then I was ushered inside on my own.

'Mum?' I called weakly towards the door, but she was long gone.

This was not right. I stood still, thumb in my mouth, my little head on one side, my little body moving side to side, swinging my skirt to and fro, and I stared at the shiny floorboards and all the other strange children careering about chasing each other.

The tall teacher came towards me, put on her kindest smile and asked: 'Would you like to come and play?'

I pulled my thumb out of my mouth and stared at her. She had very smooth skin and a long face, not nearly as welcoming as my Mum's even if she was trying her hardest to be nice.

'No!' I shouted. It was the last thing I wanted to do.

That didn't seem to make any difference and after a lot of gentle persuasion, I finally relented and joined the other noisy children. After all, there was nothing else I could do. Mum was nowhere to be seen and I supposed I had to fill in the time somehow while I waited for her to come back.

I saw the children in a group in front of the teacher doing everything she said, the silly billies. I crept round the side of the group right to the back where the teacher couldn't see me so well.

'Put your hands together and pretend you are an elephant,' she said.

This was not a good introduction for me into the world of education. Even at that tender age I wondered why on earth anyone would want to pretend to be an elephant. What a daft idea! I knew I was too small and insignificant to be able to say anything like that out loud, so I put my hands together and stretched them forward pretending to make a trunk, although even I knew a trunk was never that kind of shape, and I swung my hands to and fro with the group. What a bore.

I tolerated the day as much as I could, making half-hearted attempts to look as if I was taking part, scowling the whole time to let the teacher know I was not happy. Then, worst of all, she told us to lie down on the floor and have a rest. I watched in horror as all the children lay down and pretended to sleep. How silly! Why lie down and have a rest when you are bounding with energy? I was still raring to go. Perhaps we could go outside and have a good run? Eventually I was persuaded to follow what the other children were doing and I lay there, eyes wide open, staring at the light changing in the window as a little breeze shifted the tree branches, willing the time to pass so I could go home and be myself again.

Then, at last, we did have a little break outside. There was not much of a playground; it was just a thin strip of land to the side of the building but it had a slide. More interesting was the pile of bricks under the slide. They didn't look too heavy. I picked one up, enjoying the feeling of being alive as the rough brick edges cut into my little hand. I wondered how far I could throw it, because it was quite a weight after all. I threw it as high and as hard as I could.

'Ow!' a little boy yelled. He must have got in the way, silly boy.

I was about to pick up another brick to see if I could do better this time, but the teacher asked me to come and talk to her. It was a bit of a nuisance being interrupted when I was having fun at last, but I guessed she was in charge.

She explained that throwing bricks was not a good thing to do when there were other children who might get in the way. I shrugged my shoulders. That was life. There was definitely no fun in kindergarten.

And then, many, many years later when I was a mum myself, my little red-haired girl Jenny was taken to playgroup for the first time. I was busy working , so the child minder told me what happened. The teacher asked Jenny if she would like to come and play with the other children and Jenny just stared back, shouting: 'No!'

Does it run in families do you think?

Chapter three

Our new house at 27 Victoria Parade

We were leaving my first home in Ashgrove Street, Devonport at last. Dad had come into an inheritance and we were moving to a much posher part of Devonport. My mum was very happy.

I was only about three years old at the time and very confused, but I went along with what was happening, for that was what you did when you were the littlest in the family. We all climbed into our old Ford car and my last memory of leaving Ashgrove Street was peering through the narrow yellow plastic window at the back saying goodbye. It was very hard to see through for the thick plastic was scratched.

The new house was much bigger than our old one. It was actually two whole houses stuck together. The walls were white weatherboard and the roof made of red corrugated iron like most houses in the district. I could hardly believe that we had two of everything, including two outdoor lavatories and two verandas – one to the north where we could all sit in the sun and one to the south where my brother Peter and I could play, though it was cold and damp.

The annoying thing was that our house was still two houses – we had to go outside every time we wanted to go from one to the other. Whenever I was playing in my bedroom and felt hungry, I had to go right to the end of the hall, out through one porch and then in through the other to get to the kitchen. It was a nuisance.

Finally, Dad got so annoyed, he did something about it.

It was a night when he and Mum were having one of their parties. Everyone came to the Hammond's parties. Dad had got a whole barrel of beer and everyone had come to have a jolly good time. The hallway was absolutely full of people and it took ages for me to push past their legs to find Mum or Dad.

Eventually, I took myself to bed and listened to the laughter and shouts from all these people have a good time. I was about to doze off when I heard a tremendous thump. The whole house shook. I sat up with a start. The house was still. Perhaps I had imagined it. Then suddenly, there was another great thump. It was as though a huge elephant had stamped on our house. I thought I heard pebbles falling onto the floor, but I knew this couldn't be true. There were no pebbles inside. With a third thump, I struggled sleepily out of bed and went into the hall. There was a large crack in the wall. Another thump made the crack even bigger. I decided I would be safer in bed and went back to my room, climbed under the blankets and, in spite of the thumps and bangs and scattering of pebbles, I must have gone to sleep again.

In the morning, I crept out of bed to see what had happened. I could smell the plaster as I poked my curly little head round my bedroom door. There, right in front of me, was a huge hole in the wall and I could see though it to the other side. I woke my brother Peter and we went to look more closely. Our feet scrunched on piles of debris scattered in the hallway. They were sharper than the stones we ran over in summer, so we stepped carefully over them and then climbed through the hole and back again, hardly believing that we could at last go easily from one part of the house to the other.

The edges of the hole were jagged and snagged my nightdress, but I didn't care. This was fascinating.

The hole stayed like this for some time before Dad decided to tidy it up. He tried to cover up the pointy edges of the plaster with pieces of wood to make a kind of home-made archway. Like everything he did, it sort of worked but even I, at that tender age, knew you shouldn't be able to see some of the jagged edges above the wood. The archway stayed like that for the whole of the next ten years or so that we lived there.

Chapter four

Difficult times

I knew we were poor. Mum and Dad struggled to bring us up: my brother Peter and I. We had the usual childhood illnesses but once I was very ill. After I had the whooping cough injection, much to Mum's horror, I actually got whooping cough. I can remember hating it as I coughed and I coughed, sometimes making a great big 'whoop' before the next big coughing session. I hated the way my head filled with stars each time. I can remember lying in bed, Mum looking very worried and gently wiping my forehead with a cool cloth.

I eventually recovered but I was told I still had convulsions, or fits, sometimes when I had a high temperature. I don't remember that, although I can remember a slight feeling that something was going to happen and hearing Dad's heavy feet go down on the floor as he got out of bed to come to me. The doctor said I would outgrow it when I got older, and sure enough I had no more fits after I was about seven years old.

I often got colds and would spend days in bed until I got better. We only had the fire lit on special occasions and when I was ill in bed, this was considered a special occasion. I can remember lying in bed ill, feeling the warmth from a roaring fire in the fireplace in my room. I felt cosy and comforted as, in my fever-filled dreamy state, I glimpsed the firelight flickering on my walls. In the evenings, I would listen carefully for Dad's firm footsteps when he came in from work and asked Mum how I was.

I was in bed when the doctor came to see me. As the lavatories were outside, we had potties under our bed. My Mum kept forgetting to empty them so they got fuller and fuller. The doctor was a very tall slim man who always wore a very important-looking black striped suit. His shoes were as shiny as Dad's and he sounded very formal. I had been told that he had twelve children which I found difficult to imagine. He was taking my temperature and moving round the bed to check me when we heard a clunk and some sloshing. His large foot had found my potty! Mum was horrified, but he was a perfect gentleman and pretended nothing had happened.

Chapter five

Legacy

'Come on, Roe, you're going to a party!' Dad said.

I pulled a face. I did not want to go to a party. I was happy at home. Mum dressed me in a pretty dress and I climbed into Dad's car.

We arrived at a big hall. I wrinkled my nose as it smelt dusty. Inside there was a huge table covered with a bright table cloth and surrounded by lots of chairs. The table was stacked high with party food. I wouldn't mind tucking into the food, I thought.

'Roe meet Jilly,' Dad said, trying to introduce me to other children so that we could make friends.

'Hello', I said to the scrawny girl, briefly glancing at her and then staring at the food. Ignoring her, I went and sat at the table. My heart was set on eating those lovely cream cakes. I didn't want to make friends with strange children.

Dad put a silly party hat on me and gave me a paper plate, and at last we were allowed to eat. I tucked into cream cakes, jam sandwiches, bread with butter and hundreds and thousands, and little jam and cream filled pastry baskets. I ate and ate until I was absolutely full. The only drink was a pink cordial which I hated, but as there was nothing else, I sipped it.

'Come on children,' a strange adult said. 'Party games!'

We played Traffic Lights, where you had to run to a certain wall depending on what colour light was called and we played Statues where you had to stand very still when the music stopped playing. If you moved at all, you were out and the last one left standing won a little prize. We played Pass the Parcel where you sat in a circle holding a big well-wrapped present for a little while and then passed it on to the next person until the music stopped. Then, if you were holding the present, you could open one layer and you would get a little gift. I didn't get anything. Then we played musical chairs and the boys were too rough so I soon found I had no chair to sit on and was soon out.

My tummy felt queasy. I ran to the toilets and was sick. I hated being sick, so this year I decided I would never again eat so much at a party that I made myself sick, and I haven't.

My parents stayed at the party and later I remember being told that it was run by the Legacy – a club formed by ex-service men in the Second World War to help families who were affected by this terrible time. I didn't realise how lucky I was then, for many children's dads had been killed in the war.

It wasn't until Dad's funeral that I learned what he had been doing during the war. He had stepped in when a family needed a father figure and had come to the rescue. A nice-looking young man told me that if my father had not helped him so much, he would have gone off the rails, got into bad company and not be the man he was now. I wish I had understood that when Dad wanted me to make friends with Jilly and the other children at the party.

Chapter six

A very determined little girl

Mum always said what a determined little girl I was. My obstinacy didn't usually worry her much, and when I was older and being a naughty girl, stamping my foot and making a fuss, she used to just laugh. It was SO annoying.

However, she first found out how stubborn I was when I was only a few months old. Mothers usually try to breastfeed their babies at first and not make up bottles for them until they are older. Even in the 1940s people said that mother's milk was best. When I needed to take my first bottle, Mum went to a lot of trouble, boiling everything she could to make the glass bottle and the rubber teat sterile and heating up the milk for me to drink. She put the teat to my mouth. My little mouth remained shut. I would not open it. I screwed my face up and pushed my lips together as hard as I could. Mum tried again and again, but I would NOT give in.

'Noel!' she cried, 'I can't get this baby to take the bottle, you'll have to do it!' In sheer frustration, she thrust the stubborn baby into his arms and Dad battled with me until he finally won.

Many years later, when I was a mum myself, and your mum was only a little baby, I was exhausted from looking after her sister who was a toddler and your granddad John. – I didn't have enough milk for your mum. She needed to have a bottle and I was so tired I had to go to hospital with her. The nurse brought me a bottle of warm milk, but she wouldn't take it. I had to be very determined to win this battle against my stubborn baby so that she could grow up and be a mum herself. This was one battle I am glad I won.

And you, too, Harry, were a determined little boy. I remember once babysitting for you when you were little, and you cried and cried for your mum. Nothing would stop you. I could tell then that you are a very, very determined little boy and I am sure one day this will help you when you need it.

Chapter seven

Learning to speak properly

Let's go back to when I was about six years old, and when my determination led to another adventure. I was at school and mixing with all sorts of children. Some of them were from the back streets of Devonport, not the posh area near the River Mersey where we now lived. Mum never liked the back-street children's accents and the bad words they used, so I was sent to have elocution lessons.

Clutching my little suitcase which held a pencil and some paper, I went with Mum a little way further along Victoria Parade, the street where we lived. I liked learning, so was pleased to have a new experience even if it was on a Saturday when I usually went out to play with my friends. As we came nearer to a large white house, I tried not to think of my friends having fun playing. I could see them down at the end of the lane, playing beside the paddock. I could almost smell the new mown hay as they piled it up into little dens.

The house had a rickety gate and some big pink and blue hydrangea bushes at each side of the door. It looked welcoming. Mum undid the latch on the gate and it creaked as she opened it. We walked up the brick path and up the step to the veranda; and then we knocked on the front door. The lady who opened it looked old and kind. Mum told me she was a very special person because she could open a cigarette packet and light a cigarette with her toes. I was looking forward to seeing her do this trick, although I didn't know how it had anything to do with me learning to speak properly.

It turned out that I was here to have lessons in a sunny room on the north side of the house, learning funny poems and practising sounds. I liked the ones about a Quinquireme and about Macavity The Mystery Cat even though I wasn't exactly sure what they were all about.

One day it was announced at school there was to be a speaking competition. I was all for having a go. In those days, I was young and believed I could conquer the world. The trouble was, you had to pay an entry fee, so I asked Mum and Dad for sixpence to enter the competition. They laughed. Their little girl was always full of surprises, but this idea was silly.

I stamped my foot in a rage and shouted: 'I WILL go into the competition! I will use my OWN pocket money!' They laughed at my fury over such a tiny matter.

My elocution lessons helped me a lot. I stood at the front of the stage, speaking out loud and reading a poem my elocution teacher had taught me. I lived through the poem, acting all the time, raising my little arms in sweeping gestures. I got through to the finals.

Mum was astounded and had to go to the Town Hall to see her little girl perform again. It didn't matter that I didn't win; Mum could not laugh at me this time.

Chapter eight

Music

I was a toddler, sitting in my pushchair waiting while Mum talked to another lady outside our maroon-coloured fence in Ashgrove Street, Devonport. Mum was ALWAYS talking, often taking puffs of her cigarette in between sentences. She had lots of stories to tell that made her friends smile and laugh all the time as the minutes slipped by.

I hadn't learnt to talk yet. I didn't understand words but I found the rise and fall of Mum's voice fascinating, and with my head on one side I listened. I could speak like that too. I mimicked the sounds of her conversation, my little voice rising and falling in excited bursts that just sounded like Mum's. It was fun.

Suddenly Mum stopped mid-sentence. Her friend was laughing loudly, pointing at me, joking and saying that perhaps Mum had been talking too much for I was joining in. Mum looked at her little daughter. I stopped and looked up. I didn't understand what all the fuss was about, but it was good to know that they were interested. Mum laughed and resumed her stream of funny stories. It didn't stop her talking; nothing could stop Mum talking and that's how we all liked it. One of my cousins once said that she called Mum 'The Gurgly Lady' because Mum was always laughing.

Sounds interested me right from the beginning. I learned many years later that music is just 'organised sound' and music became my life. I joined in all the singing at kindergarten and in school. I happily joined in 'Incy Wincy Spider' doing the actions with great gusto. I loved it. At home I taught myself the recorder and held little concerts. I arranged all the children's chairs we had in little rows on our veranda on the cold side of the house, ignoring the strong smell of damp. I invited the neighbours to come and listen to me playing 'God save the Queen' on the recorder. I can still see poor Mrs Webb, our next-door neighbour and a very large cuddly woman, squashed into a tiny cane chair, her body overflowing the seat at an alarming rate. She was the only member of the audience. She was always very kind to me, so kind that whenever I could, I popped next door to see her and ask if she had anything for me. She always had a little box of trinkets that I could take home and play with. When Mum found me doing this, she said that I must stop asking for things, so after that I just talked to Mrs Webb over the fence.

No one knew where my musical ability came from until I inherited a very old piano book from my grandmother Lillian Graham– the name of Dad's mum before she married. The book contained a lot of very difficult piano exercises. However, Mum and Dad had no musical ability at all.

Dad told me that when he was at the Hutchins School in Hobart, all the boys were lined up and told to sing. The music master walked along the rows of pupils and listened. When he came to Dad, he listened for a while, pointed at Dad and said 'Out!'. Dad couldn't even sing in tune! Mum told me that she was supposed to go to piano lessons but didn't want to, so she never turned up. Her step-mum didn't know anything about this until she met the piano teacher in the street in Hobart. The piano teacher said how sorry she was that Florence was ill so often. Mum got into a lot of trouble with her step-mum but she didn't have to pretend to go to her piano lessons any more.

I, on the other hand, at the age of six declared that I wanted, I REALLY wanted to learn the piano. I also wanted a pony and a big dolls' house, but piano lessons were most important. Mum said that she and Dad couldn't afford to pay for the lessons. By then I had realised that we were very poor. I remember we could only have cream occasionally because it was so expensive and lunch, when I came home from school, was mainly bread, butter and jam. I had to wait until I was eleven before I could start learning the piano. That was when Mum went to work as the police magistrate's secretary.

I was very excited when I went for my first piano lesson with Renee Newman. I loved it and was soon playing tunes with both hands. I remember 'The Jolly Farmer' and 'The Blue Danube Waltz'. When the neighbours knew that I had started learning the piano, they gave me lots of music and I devoured it all.

Then came the Devonport Eisteddfod held in Devonport Town Hall – a very tall and imposing building. I had learnt the pieces off my heart. As I listened to other children going on stage one after the other, I thought 'I can play that piece much better'. I wasn't nervous. It was eventually my turn.

I walked smartly onto the stage, sat at the piano and played away almost in a dream just as I did at home. Then, suddenly, I stopped. My heart started hammering. I had forgotten the rest of the piece. I had no idea what the next notes could be. My fingers trembled as I tried again, stopping again at the same spot. My heart got louder and louder, my hands started sweating. It was the end of the world. I was about to run from the stage when I heard the judge's booming voice bellow from the floor above.

'For goodness sake someone give her the music!' he roared. No one moved.

'Here,' he yelled, 'take mine!' and he threw his copy down to the stalls where someone picked it up and while I sat rigid on the piano stool, they brought it to me. I stumbled through the piece to the end. As soon as I had finished, I rushed off the stage in tears. The judge said that this was the best performance yet but that did little to dent my absolute misery.

I had to play the piano in public many times over the years to come. I always felt very nervous, but I knew that was just one of those things. If I wanted to have somewhere to live and food on the table, I had to have a career. I just had to get on with it and stop my nerves winning every time I played. I learned to practise the music until I knew every note so well that I could play it automatically and my fingers could play even if my thoughts were in a muddle.

Chapter nine

The Queen

It was 1952 and I was about 5five years old. I had just got used to the school routine. In the morning we would march out to assemble in the playground. The lucky older children took it in turns to bang a big drum for us to march to their solid beat. When we were all in a line and most of us had stopped talking after many glares, hand signals and barking from our teachers, the headmaster appeared.

He was called Mr Ferguson. He was so tall. He always wore a thin striped suit which made him seem very important and rather scary. He walked towards the front of our line very firmly, his heavy footsteps echoing in the playground. As I stretched my neck and stared up into the sky, I could just see his face. I had to look up even higher as he climbed onto the bench in front of us. The bench was one we often sat on at playtime and it only had thin wooden slats. I often waited with bated breath, waiting for his feet to go through the bench, but they never did.

However, today, there was no assembly in the playground. We were all marched across the school grounds to the path outside where we all stood waiting for someone important. Our teacher thrust a flag at each of us and we stood clutching our Union Jacks. We had been told something about the flag by our teacher, – something about one cross belonging to St George, another one to St Andrew and that they were both stuck together.

Suddenly we were told to cheer and wave our flags, so we did, not being exactly sure why we were doing this. A loud motor bike came along and then a big long car with its hood down rushed past. I thought I saw a little person inside waving gently back at us, but I couldn't be sure. I found out later it was the Queen. There were pictures of her all over our school. She was a slim lady in a posh dress with a blue sash and she had a little crown on her head. She looked like a nice lady although she was not the friendly sort you could join at the kitchen table and listen to telling her stories like Mum. I was used to the Queen being part of our school lives, but I never really understood why. However, it made an exciting school morning for us.

Even more excitement came at home when Mum realised the Queen was going to be driven past our house. She was going to be driven along the Esplanade that ran all along the river to town. Our place had a drive that went all the way down to the Esplanade. How amazing!

Mum asked all her friends to come and see her too and, of course, we had to have a picnic on the lawn. Dad did his best to put up some flags around our gate at the bottom of the drive and we all hung around the gate waiting to see her. I could see her gloved hand a little better this time and there was a man next to her in the car. I was told he was the Duke of Edinburgh.

We all did our waving and cheering, Mum doing the most, and then we went back to the lawn for our picnic. The fact that the lawn was a bit bumpy and that the picnic consisted mostly of salad bread rolls held together with rubber bands didn't stop Mum and her friends enjoying themselves while I listened quietly to their chatter.

During that time there were a lot of very important people in Devonport and one of them called in at our local pub. Dad went down to the pub most evenings and never bothered to change. Everyone knew who he was and so there was no need to dress up; after all, he was relaxing. Mum was horrified when he told her after one visit that the Governor General had popped into the pub and had been chatting to Dad.

'And you were wearing your gardening clothes!' Mum had said, horrified.

'Yes and why not?' Dad had replied. Sometimes there was no moving Dad.

Years later I was in Launceston when the Queen visited again. This time she was on walkabout and I saw her up close. I remember being amazed at how short she is and equally amazed that the Duke of Edinburgh was wearing make-up! I mean, a MAN wearing make-up! I'd never heard of it.

Even later still when Dad was on TV speaking on behalf of the Chamber of Commerce, he had had to have powder put on his nose so that it didn't shine. Nowadays when they film outside so much, they often forget and when I see someone speaking who has a shiny nose, I mutter at the screen 'Who forgot to put powder on his nose?'

Chapter ten

Candles

He was a short stumpy little dog with a short stumpy tail and a face that looked like a pensive old man, but he was our dog, our friend in time of need and a member of the family who gave us lots of fun.

It was warm enough in Australia for him to be an outside dog. He had his little kennel if he felt cold, but most of the time he wandered happily around the yard or even out along our streets. We didn't need to take him for a walk – he took himself and no one seemed to mind.

Whenever we had ice creams, we had to get one for Candles. We would prop it up between two stones and he would lick the ice cream again and again until it was all gone.

He liked to take an interest in everything. We also had a cat, Mandy, who was a little aloof from Candles, but I guess you could say they were friends. Mandy often had kittens. It was fascinating watching her produce one kitten after another and then see them drink from her and grow day by day. When they were six weeks old, we had to find homes for them. Mum knew a lot of people in Devonport and soon the kittens would be taken away, one by one. I was horrified when our sports teacher at school told me she was going to have two of our kittens. How embarrassing! Every time we had games, Cormie, the teacher, would tell me about them. All the other girls would stare at me. Was I trying to curry favour with the teacher?

One day, just after Mandy had had another batch of kittens, Candles walked out onto the porch and with something in his mouth.

I screamed, 'Candles is killing the kittens!'

Mum rushed out and went to Candles. The kitten was unharmed. 'He is just trying to be a father to them,' Mum explained.

Another time it was reported that Devonport football team had a new mascot: a little black and white dog who rushed out onto the field in front of the team before the match started. We soon realised it was Candles!

He came with us when we moved house to 3 Nicholls Street and enjoyed sleeping in the sun. He eventually became too old and lay under the oak tree. The vet was called and we were told Candles died of kidney failure.

We didn't plan to have another dog, but we accidentally acquired a stray that Mum called 'Wog'. She thought his previous owners had called him 'Dog' for that was the only word that he responded to.

Chapter eleven

My bedroom at Victoria Parade

Peter and I were very lucky for we had a bedroom each. Mine was done up in pink with matching bedspread and curtains which must have been lovely at first, but as the years passed I got used to the mould on the curtains. There was no central heating in those days. Most rooms had a fireplace which usually remained unlit.

I was a bit of a fidget and always rushing around, chewing my cheek or winding my hair round and round my finger. The plaster on the wall next to my bed had a little crack and it was not long before I had picked out a lot of the plaster to reveal the wooden struts that had held it in place. I don't remember the hole I had created ever getting fixed. It didn't matter.

I found at the back of the north veranda there was a hole in the floor where some of the struts had broken. One day I climbed through the hole to find flat earth underneath. I liked the strong smell of dirt and discovered that the floor was high enough for me to make a little cubby hole under the veranda. I often took my books and a candle, and spent time reading in this secretive dark place. It was wonderful. There was one day when there was a strange smell, stronger than the dirt. It was a smoky sort of smell. I realised just in time that I had set my hair alight! I slammed my book onto the spot on my head and the fire went out, although the air was still full of the horrid acrid smell. I didn't think about any dangers when I was there. Tasmania also has a number of very venomous spiders like the Redback and there were lots of cobwebs I had to sweep aside as I clambered underneath the old slats in the floor.

Unlike the cool darkness underneath the floorboards, it was very sunny and hot above them. We used to sit in our chairs and daydream in the sun. It was too hot to do anything else. One day I was on this veranda by myself when a lot of little lizards slipped up the stone steps and in jerky little steps dashed across the slats to join me. They loved the sun too. I slid off my chair and lay on the floor watching them as they sat still lifting their little heads to soak in the sun. More and more gathered on the veranda with me until there was hardly a space to move. I picked up one of the lizards by its tail and held it closer to see what its little eyes were like. To my amazement, the beast dropped to the floor, leaving its thin slimy tail dangling between my fingers. The lizard dashed away unharmed except for missing a tail. Wow! I'd never seen anything like this before. I did this again in a mesmerised dream hardly believing what was happening.

Chapter twelve

Manfern, leeches, jack jumpers and snakes

Opposite the steps to the hot sunny veranda was a huge tree always in the shade from next door's fence. I thought it was a tree for it had a very thick trunk and had leaves like a fern. Dad told me later that is was not a tree, but a Manfern. I put my arms around its huge trunk and felt how soft and damp it was. It had a jungle sort of smell. It was definitely different to a normal tree.

A friend told me there is a difference between a Manfern and a Tree Fern but I cannot remember what it is. They both look the same to me –like massive ferns that have grown into trees. They are very special plants in Tasmania which is only one of about three places in the whole world where you can find fossilised Tree Fern. A Tree Fern fossilises when it falls down and dies, staying where it is for so long that it turns to stone. I have a piece of fossilised Tree Fern from Tasmania that is 180 million years old – from the period of time called the Jurassic period when dinosaurs wandered the earth.

When we went exploring in the bush, sometimes there were very damp jungle-like places. There were little waterfalls that looked lovely but from the trees next to them little black slimy creatures would drop and crawl under your blouse or shirt, and suck your blood until they were full. Then they dropped off. These were leeches. You didn't feel them sucking your blood because they injected something that stopped you feeling what they were doing.

One time we visited Cradle Mountain, a huge mountain that must have been an enormous volcano once, and we went on a walk in a damp forest. I was fascinated by the mounds of moss and the red mushrooms with white dots – just like the pictures in the story books. When we came to the wooden shelter built for wanderers like us, we found out that we had all been attacked by leeches. We took off all the clothes we could and helped each other, even strangers, get the leeches off by lighting a match and pushing it against them or putting salt where they were attached to our skin. I had had eleven leeches on me!

Other annoying creatures were jack jumpers. These are medium-sized ants with yellow pincers at the front of their bodies. One day when I was about six, I was sitting on a tree trunk, listening to the sounds of the bush and watching the sun filter through the dry gum trees. I was happy, relaxed and on holiday, and had time to revel in the smell of dry bark and gum tree leaves.

Suddenly I felt a stabbing pain in my toes. I looked down and there was a crowd of black jack jumpers, some of them using their horrible yellow pincers to squeeze my toes as if to eat me. I screamed and screamed, and shook my foot violently, but they would not come off. I hobbled towards the little wooden shack where we were staying, screaming all the time. Dad came out and had to take the horrid little creatures off one by one. It was awful.

When I am in bare feet or even when I am wearing sandals, to this day I look down at my feet to make sure there are no jack jumpers thinking of having me for a meal.

There is another good reason for looking down at your feet in Tasmania. When I was a very little girl, Dad always told Peter and I to look at our feet, especially when we were walking in long grass. We had to watch out for snakes. There are three venomous snakes in Tasmania: the Tiger Snake, the Brown Snake and the Copperhead. They could all kill you if they bit you. Dad told us that if we left them alone, they would leave us alone, but if you accidentally trod on one … we didn't want to think about it, so whenever we were walking towards a grassy paddock, I can hear Dad's voice calling out 'Watch your feet!'

One day, Dad, Peter and I were walking along a narrow path towards the beach on a farm where we were holidaying. On either side of the path was long, dry grass. Dad went first, carrying our towels, then me and then Peter. I kept turning around to taunt my brother, something I did quite often, when suddenly Dad pushed me roughly aside. I shouted a protest, but was glad when I saw what he had seen. He dropped the towels and reached for a very heavy stick, and bashed the ground again and again just where I had been about to step. It was a snake! Dad had done what you are supposed to do when you meet a venomous snake. He had dropped what he had in his hands to distract the snake and then bashed its backbone until it was broken and could not move or attack us.

When I was a Girl Guide many years later, we were told that if a friend of ours has been bitten by one of these snakes, we should cut the wound open with a sharp knife, suck out the poison in the blood and spit it out. Then we were told to put a tourniquet above the wound. This meant tying something very tight around their arm or leg above where they had been bitten. This would stop the blood flowing and so stop the venom from getting into your system. Nowadays, I think they only talk about putting the tourniquet on.

Chapter thirteen

Enjoying solitude

My brother Peter and I were SO different that we rarely played together. I enjoyed the peace and quiet alone.

Besides creeping under the veranda floor to read by candlelight, I also climbed onto the rickety roof of the shed where the lavatories were opposite the house. The roof was covered with vines and I hollowed out a little cubby hole, wriggled inside and read to my heart's content. It was a lovely position to see everyone who came down Walpole Lane – the narrow unsurfaced road that ran behind our house. The lane was full of cobble stones and was very rough to walk or drive on so very few people came down it and my reading was rarely interrupted.

The shed walls were also quite dilapidated and the wooden panels had gaps in between them where you could see the daylight. One day I looked and there was a blue-tongued lizard! He was a little fat pale-yellow-coloured lizard the size of the palm of my hand and when he stuck out his tongue, it was blue. Mum suggested I left a saucer of milk for him and sure enough, after I put the saucer down in front of a gap in the shed wall, a little head poked through the hole and I could watch its blue tongue lapping up the milk.

I had my own special playroom on the north side of the house. All my toys were scattered over the floor. Sometimes I would gather a lot of empty packets and stack them up to play shops. At other times I would line up all the dolls and pretend to be a teacher. I would spend many happy hours there with these toys and our cat Mandy. She was a lovely fluffy grey and white cat who purred every time I stroked her.

Chapter fourteen

The Mardi Gras

At Easter time, Devonport was buzzing with excitement. We were having a Mardi Gras and it would be held on Victoria Parade.

We were very lucky because our house was just up from where they were going to hold the Mardi Gras so they had to let us in for free. I went on my own, every day, clutching my pocket money in my hand and had a go at all the stalls.

The one I liked best was the table with upturned bottle tops with numbers in them. If you threw your coin onto the dead centre of one of the coins, you got your coin back and if you managed to throw your coin onto the dead centre of one that was coloured red, you got double your money back. I used to treble my pocket money that way, but I knew I couldn't rely on this happening every time and sometimes I lost.

I had a go at shooting the ducks and plopping the ping pong balls down the throats of china clown heads as they turned from side to side. I sat on a horse in the carousel and watched the people as I went round and round. I bought some pink candy floss and let it coat my nose. I didn't care. It was great fun.

Finally, I leant over our wrought-iron gate and watched the parade of different floats filled with people I recognised from town dressed up in silly clothes.

Chapter fifteen

Saturdays

Every Saturday Dad got out his cylinder lawn mower and, pushing it by hand, mowed our big lawn. He had to mow all the way down to the end of the drive too, making sure he didn't chop off the blue iris heads that stood to attention on either side. He didn't like all this hard work. He had enough to do at the office.

Then Mum and Dad had a brilliant idea. They would get an animal like a goat or a sheep to stand on the lawn and eat all the grass so Dad would no longer have to do any mowing.

Soon there was a sheep standing bewildered on our lawn. She did as she should; she happily chewed away at the long grass and little by little it appeared as though it had been very closely mown. However, she was lonely; she needed to be with her mates. She stood outside Mum and Dad's bedroom which overlooked the lawn and bleated – not just once or twice, but ALL the time, day and night.

Mum complained that she couldn't sleep. Eventually, the sheep had to go and Dad reluctantly got out the mower again.

Saturday was also the time when I often went to the cinema with my friends. We walked into town and queued outside the cinema for tickets. I always liked to go upstairs and look at the huge screen from the balcony. After getting the tickets, we bought our sweets and the ones I liked the best were Minties (little square chewy mint-tasting sweets in wrappers which had jokes printed on them), Liquorice Allsorts and Jaffas (little round balls of chocolate coated with a crunchy orange covering.)

Once the film started, it was completely dark in the cinema. Once when I was feeling hungry, I shoved my hand into the box of Jaffas as I stared at the news that had just started on the screen, but I missed the box and it fell from my fingers and dropped to the ground. The sweet little round balls began to spill out of the container. I pretended it had nothing to do with me as I listened to the drop, drop of every single sweet as it bounced step by step all the way down to the front of the balcony.

We loved the films. They were all in black and white, and even though I thought the news was boring, the films were new and exciting. After the news were trailers of the films that would be on in the next few weeks and then came the main film which was usually about cowboys and Indians.

Chapter sixteen

Coswell

There was a place on the south-east coast of Tasmania called Coswell. It was a small farm of very dry grass scattered with stones that could have been there for centuries. At the end of the farm was a long beach of pure sand – sand that had rarely been touched by humans and sand that stretched down to a clear sparkling sea full of fish. It was all ours when we went there on holiday.

Dad had been told by the doctor that if he didn't have a holiday, he would die soon. So Dad decided that we should have three weeks' holiday at the beach.

When he was a young boy he would go on holiday to Coswell with a lot of other youngsters and be looked after by Tooey (the housekeeper) and Wally Donne (the owner of the farm). The name Donne is famous because of a very well-known poet, John Donne. I found out much later that Wally was a descendant of a cousin of the poet. However, Wally didn't go in for poetry much, but I do remember him as a very kind man with a dog that kept curling round his legs. They wanted me to make friends with the dog, but I had been bitten by one before and I was too frightened.

Our summer in Australia is in December and January and this was when we packed up our little car, a grey Standard, climbed in and set off from Devonport to go over the hills and through the mountains until we arrived at Swansea, a little town near Coswell.

The little car was not very strong and we always had to stop on the top of a mountain for its radiator to cool down. I would get out and explore the tiny waterfalls that dribbled down the sharp grey rocks of the mountain. I breathed in the pure cool air and, being careful not to go too near the edge of the road, peered down the steep slope thinly covered in straggly trees and gum. The scanty pieces of earth on top of some of the rocks above me were bedecked with brightly coloured pink heath. I loved it.

As we neared Swansea, we all looked out for the vanishing house and I was invariably the first one to spot it. It would suddenly appear as we rounded the bend coming down from the hills towards the coast.

It was a bit of a bother putting up Dad's tents for they were made of canvas and were like the ones he used in the army. They had an inner sheet that I was told, again and again, not to touch because if that sheet touched the outside of the tent it would leak and although nearly every day was sunny and hot, occasionally it rained and rained hard.

Peter, my brother, and I shared a tent, and we would lie on our camp beds in the warm evenings and talk. One day we were trying to make up a new language when Mum called out:

'Why don't you use the language we used to use.'

We were interested.

'All you have to do,' she continued, 'is, instead of saying "bed" you say "bub e dud", doubling the consonants.' For the next hour or so our conversation was very strange, but we were happy and entertained. There was no TV in those days and we didn't even bring a wireless, although Dad had his newspaper every morning. He sat in his pyjamas outside the tent, seated on a canvas chair, his Australian digger's hat firmly on his head and he read the newspaper, cover to cover.

When we felt like it, after breakfast, the hot water for Mum and Dad's tea boiled in a billy can over a fire, Peter and I would go out to play. Peter and I were SO different that we often played alone.

I explored the beach feeling special with no one else in sight. I breathed in the salty air and followed the edge of the sea, my bare feet feeling cool as I trod on the wet sand. I took no notice of the strong sun burning my skin. Blisters on my nose and shoulders were to be expected every summer. I was looking for interesting shells, the sparkling white cuttlefish that the budgerigars liked or shark eggs which were hollow shiny black pockets. Sometimes I would stop to pop the seaweed.

One day I walked round the headland and found a beach full of cowrie shells. They were delicate little shells, soft and brown in colour, with little smoothly serrated mouths. They were all different sizes and different browns from almost pink to a deep brown. I loved visiting this beach. Like a lone shipwreck survivor, I wandered along the shore, treading on my shadow as it crossed the line of shells on the damp sand when the sea had just retreated. I collected shell after shell, ignoring my burning shoulders as I moved slowly forward, bending every now and again to add to my collection. On one of my visits to this beach I had collected 70 of the little shells. My teacher had told me that they were once used for money. I smiled as I thought of the shoe box in my cupboard at home, full of treasure. I now had a hundred of the pretty round things.

On another occasion, I found a fascinating gypsy caravan. It was painted green and had big steps up to its wooden door. I stepped up to it and knocked. The door swung open and there was a kind-looking old gentleman.

'Hello' he said, as I tried to peer round him and see what was inside. 'Would you like to see my collection of aboriginal flints and axeheads?'

I slipped inside, my eyes soon getting accustomed to the darkness. On benches all round the caravan were stones of all sizes. The aborigines had made them by hitting two stones together until a piece was knocked off, leaving a sharp edge.

Every day while this lovely old gentleman, a dentist, had his holiday, we walked the paddocks of the farm, searching for flints and axe heads. We found a lot of flints but alas no axe heads. Dr Bennett, for that was his name, showed me how you could recognise the stones that the aborigines had cut to scrape off the skin from any animals they had caught for food, such as kangaroos, wallabies or possums.

I was fascinated by the different world that the aborigines must have lived in when they had no cars or houses; they just lived in the wild with little food or shelter. It must have been very hard.

Dr Bennett told me how the white man (us) had come and tried to help the aborigines by giving them food, but all we did was bring disease and too much sugar so that the aborigines' white teeth, made strong by the charcoal of cooked meat, were spoiled by sugar and lack of cleaning.

The Tasmanian aborigines were black, much blacker than the mainland ones, for the Tasmanians came from Micronesia, an area in the Pacific Ocean down through the mainland and across Bass Strait that had been land at that time. The mainland abos, as we call them, came from Macronesia and were a more browny colour.

There are no full-blooded Tasmanian aborigines left. The last one, Truganini, died in the early twentieth century. Some people still have Tasmanian blood in them including one of the girls who went to school with me in Hobart who said that her grandmother had had aboriginal blood in her. I didn't remind her that in one generation in the future someone could have a black baby as a result and would have a lot of explaining to do.

At first the English tried to be fair and I remember seeing a poster they had put up with pictures that showed a white man killing an aborigine and that white man being hanged and an aborigine killing a white man with the aborigine being hanged.

There are terrible tales that the Englishmen tried to kill all the abos. They formed a line across the centre of Tasmania and moved forward down to the south coast killing every aborigine they saw. Luckily, they failed because the land is so big, almost two-thirds the size of England, so they didn't have enough soldiers to do the job.

'Let's go fishing,' Dad said one day and he took my brother and me out in the rickety rowing boat. 'See those seagulls over there?'

I nodded.

'We'll go and fish there, for that's where there will be the most fish. The seagulls know.'

Dad was right.

He helped put bait on the painful hooks and showed us how to sling the thin green fishing lines over the edge. My line was the first to wriggle. Again and again we pulled up our fishing lines, a fish on each hook. We had caught hundreds of them. The fish were nearly all flathead. I can still feel the thrill of such a good catch.

Chapter seventeen

My granddad, Bertram Samuel Hammond

He was Dad's father. He came out from Yorkshire, England, as a missionary priest to live in Tasmania at a place called Bothwell and Dad was brought up in a vicarage. That's why Dad wouldn't go to church if he could help it – he had had to go to so many services with his father in charge of the church that he got fed up with the whole thing. He did get married to Mum in a church, however, and my granddad took the service. When he came to the bit where he says 'and my worldly goods I thee endow' Granddad winked at Dad. He knew Dad didn't really have any worldly goods to give Mum.

When Dad was living in the rectory in Bothwell, near the centre of Tasmania, he would sometimes play with his sister in the snow. His mum was having another baby and they were very excited. Sadly, after giving birth to Dad's little brother, his mum became very pale and ill, and died. It was very sad so some years later Dad acquired a step-mum instead. We called her Aunty Ellie and she had a very different way of speaking. When she spoke, she had a strange whine to her voice that Mum used to imitate perfectly.

Granddad was very tall and I remember craning my little neck to see his face. He was a dark, thin, imposing figure that frightened me a little. He wouldn't let anyone say anything bad about his home in England – Yorkshire. I remember him when he lived at the Hagley Church on the road to Hobart.

One day he showed me where they kept the bread for communion and I was allowed to have a piece. I rolled it around my mouth and thought how dry it was. The freshly cooked bread that Mum used to bring home from the Devonport bakery was much nicer.

Later Granddad gave me hundreds of stamps he had collected, including some of the old Tasmanian ones, although these have since been lost in the mists of time, like a lot of other things I wish I had kept. Dad used to collect stamps too, and he had a triangular one from South Africa that was very special. When my brother was very young, he wanted to make friends with one of the boys at Scouts, so he gave him some of Dad's stamps including this South African one. Dad was not pleased.

I should not talk badly about my brother for I was a bit of a naughty girl too. When we children had done something wrong, Dad would get cross, so Peter and I hid behind the door while he was shouting. I giggled which made everything worse. Dad would then get very, very cross and punish Peter. I should have said it was my fault, but I didn't and I feel very bad about it now. Do you think it's too late for me to say sorry?

Chapter eighteen

Primary school

I was in a classroom with a lot of other children. There were four of us sitting round a little table with a lady who was helping us read. The book was boring – about Pat and Jan, I think, who had very boring lives. Even the grass was a plain green without any light and shade. Everything was repeated so many times. It was only years later that I realised that that was how the book was helping us learn to read the words.

I loved playtime and quite happily drank the little bottle of milk we were given. Then I would run around chasing the others. I would often fall down onto the asphalt playground and cut me knee. I just ignored it and eventually it would heel. Once I got some grit in the cut and I decided to leave it to see what would happen. I still have a slightly dark coloured line on my knee to this day as a result.

One of my teachers in the primary school was Miss Lawrence. She was tall, slim and had this amazing head of curly, red hair. Her skin was pale and dotted with freckles, the black clothes she wore making her look like a witch, even though she was not nearly as old as Mrs Webb from next door.

Miss Lawrence was our teacher for the year and we were all very frightened of her. In the olden days teachers were allowed to use the cane, and my word, Miss Lawrence was ALWAYS hitting one of us with hers. The cane was a long thin piece of round wood that she waved about in a threatening manner as she talked to us in her shrill, high-pitched voice. She moved swiftly and jerkily round the classroom, wielding her cane like a weapon that she was always on the brink of using. Every now and then, suddenly, when she saw a naughty boy kicking his legs or tapping his friend on the shoulder, she would lift her cane high and bring it down with a tremendous 'thwack' on his legs, and then as he tried to make his escape, she hit him again and again on the back of his legs and chased him to the back of the classroom. We cowered over our desks praying she would not pick on us next.

One day, she told us something strange. Well I thought it was strange at the time, but in the tense, frightening atmosphere of the classroom, you didn't ask any questions; you just did exactly as you were told in case you got the cane. We were very, very careful in her class for we had to get everything absolutely right.

We were learning about the seasons.

'Write the heading on the left,' she said as she pointed her cane to the words 'The Seasons', showing us her very carefully shaped heading in white chalk on the black board.

I very slowly and cautiously printed the words 'The Seasons' on the left of the page, squeezing them in behind the margin. She prowled the room glaring at every pupil's work, making sure they were doing just what she asked. I could hear her bark some cross words at a boy behind me. He had smudged his page with his dirty hands.

Suddenly I jumped as she yelled in my ear, 'What on earth are you doing?'

I lowered my head and glanced upwards at her angry face.

'You should have put the heading here!' She stabbed her cane at the centre of my page. 'Get to the front of the classroom, you silly girl. You will get the cane!'

I slowly slid out of my chair and crept to the front of the room, staring at my class mates who sent me waves of sympathy. My knees trembled as my heart thumped louder and louder.

'Hold out your hand!' she snarled.

I closed my eyes tight and stretched my sweaty hand out as far from me as I could. I tensed every muscle, took in a huge breath and waited. Every tiny moment was unbearable. Finally, I heard her breathe in deeply and after a short, agonising pause, thwack! She slammed her cane hard onto the palm of my hand. It hurt; it really hurt. I held my burning hand onto my chest and fought back the tears. I would not cry; she wasn't going to make me cry. I slunk in my seat and snivelled. I didn't like Miss Lawrence.

At home that night, I blurted out how unhappy we were in Miss Lawrence's class, how nearly everyone had got the cane, including me, and how when one of the boys in particular ever made the slightest wrong move, she would lash into him, yelling at the top of her voice. She had a temper, a very quick temper and we suffered.

Dad listened intently to my story and was very cross. He told me he would write a letter to the headmaster. A few days later I noticed a change in Miss Lawrence. Although she still used the cane, she used it much less than before. She was especially careful when she spoke to me. I enjoyed a small feeling of triumph which I am ashamed to say I used to my advantage.

It was while I was in her class that I sprained the wrist on my right hand, my writing hand. I had fallen on it in the playground and it hurt. A few moments later my wrist became very swollen. When Mum saw this, she took me to the doctor. I had a real injury! I was important at last. Although it hurt a bit, it didn't hurt THAT much, but I really enjoyed being made a fuss of. I smiled inside as I knew I wouldn't get into trouble from Miss Lawrence about my writing any more because I couldn't write, I had to rest my arm until it was better. I sat smugly at my desk, my right arm in a sling and my left hand free to turn the pages of Enid Blyton's *Omnibus*. I loved reading Enid Blyton and I read her stories again and again while out of the corner of my eye I could see my classmates struggle through the anxious day's work. Eventually, I knew my arm was better, but I pretended that it still hurt.

'Ooh no, I couldn't use it without it hurting,' I said one day, thinking I would read the story about the Brownie next – the one where she was hiding in her horse costume on the stage munching chocolate biscuits she knew she shouldn't eat. I loved that story the best, because it was just the sort of thing I would do.

Miss Lawrence looked at me turning over the page.

'Rosemary,' she said in a kind voice I hadn't heard before. 'Your wrist has been bad for a very long time; don't you think you should try to write now?'

What could I say? The game was up. I knew it had been better for ages so I very slowly slid my perfectly healed wrist out of its sling acting as if it was very hard to do, and very slowly put my pencil on the paper and started forming the letters, mouthing them as I spelled them out in my head. Oh, how I had enjoyed my little break, but now I had to say goodbye to Enid Blyton and return to the anxious times ahead until next year when we would get a new teacher.

Chapter nineteen

Pretending to be a duck-billed platypus

When I was a tubby six-year old I was a Brownie and wore the brown uniform and yellow tie with pride. I was minding my own business one day, when I was suddenly told to go to Mrs Todd's which was a few houses up Nicholls St, just around the corner from us.

She measured me, fat tummy and all, and that was when I discovered I had been chosen to be the duck-billed platypus to welcome a very important person who was visiting us. I was told it would be Lady Baden-Powell, the wife of Lord Baden-Powell who set up the Scouts. Later, girls were allowed to form their own club called the Guides and I became a Guide when I was older.

So, one sunny afternoon, wearing my best Brownie uniform, I lay myself face down on the dry grass and pulled my duck-billed platypus costume over my head. When Lady Baden-Powell came near me, I was to push a little message through the pretend bill. That sounded fine, because she wouldn't see me.

The ground was a bit smelly, but I didn't mind. I waited and waited, fingering the piece of paper with the fingers of my right hand.

Finally, as I peeked under my unusual cover, I saw a sturdy pair of legs in thick stockings and solid black shoes with thick heels. I knew this was Lady Baden-Powell. The feet shuffled closer and closer. Finally, she was directly in front of me. I pushed the letter through and waited with bated breath. Would she see it? Would she take it?

To my horror, suddenly I found myself exposed to the bright sunshine. She had lifted my costume right up revealing my plump little body squirming to get out of sight. I grabbed my costume hurriedly, saying:

'You are not SUPPOSED to do that. I was supposed to give you the letter through my bill.'

She laughed, admired me and the costume, and took the letter. I pulled the costume back down over me, making sure I was completely covered up again and glowered underneath.

I have never quite learnt how to behave properly when important people are around.

I did see a real duck-billed platypus once. They are very shy creatures, I was told. I was a university student helping as a volunteer at a monastery on the Atherton Tableland in Queensland where it is very hot and the roads and fields are full of big black cane toads. You got used to the toads after a while for they didn't hurt you if you didn't hurt them, although I wasn't very pleased when someone left one in my bed! yuk!

One day, one of the monks said he would show us where we could see a duck-billed platypus. Never having seen one before, I was keen to go, so we climbed into a ramshackle truck and we were driven to a lake further inland. I was expecting the water to be clear and blue, but it was very muddy and a light-brown colour. Then we saw it, a tiny bit of black bill gliding through the water. I pretended to be excited and interested, but that was not my idea of seeing one for real. I expected to see the whole creature creeping down to the lake and slipping in, but that was not to be.

Back at primary school many years earlier, a new girl had arrived. She was Cora Helleman and she had come from Holland. She spoke no English at first, but after a few months she was speaking normally. As I was walking home from our little primary school on the top of the hill, she was on the same path and going towards her home which was only around the corner from mine.

We became best friends and I went round to her place nearly every night. Our families were so different. My mum was very relaxed and laughed all the time. There was hardly any routine at home and I could do what I wanted when I wanted. Cora's mum was quite serious, very organised and made the children do what they were told. Her brother was often clipped around the ears for being naughty. When Cora came home from school, she would have a glass of milk and some biscuits ready for her. I often stayed for tea and Fridays was really special because it was cooking day and her Mum often made a gorgeous apple and cinnamon cake. I could smell the cinnamon at the gate as soon as we arrived, so I ran down the path lined with yellow marigolds. Everything was in order; at home everything was in disorder and I loved the contrast.

Cora and I competed with each other all the time. She was very good at languages, and because of Cora, I wanted to do languages too and at high school I studied French, German and Latin.

Chapter twenty

Using ink pens

Just after Cora had arrived at the primary school, our class was learning to use ink.

We had mastered how to use a pencil and to write all our letters and even to write with joined-up writing, but now it was time to use ink.

We were not allowed to have fountain pens or biros in those days.

We sat at little wooden desks. You could lift the top of the desk up and there, inside, you could keep all your exercise books and pencils. Now we also had a bottle of ink, a blotter and some pens. The pens were thin pieces of wood in the shape of pencils which had been scraped at the bottom with a little slit into which you pushed a brassy metal nib. I hated doing that because the nib was so sharp that it stuck into your finger leaving black marks. We poured some ink into a special little hole with a container at the top of our desk.

It was very difficult. Once we had put the pen together we dipped the nib into the ink and started writing with it. After every word or so, you had to remember to blot the ink dry or it would smudge. Of course, my first efforts were full of smudges and blots of ink when too much ink fell onto the paper while I was trying to write.

Thank goodness we were allowed to use real fountain pens and biros later in our school lives.

Chapter twenty-one

Grandpa Seager and meeting my soulmate

Grandpa Seager, my mum's dad, lived in Hobart, for that was where Mum was born and raised. Grandpa Seager and Mum's step-mum lived in a large house on the hill in Dynnyrne. The house was dark and when we stepped into the tiny kitchen there was a strong smell of gas. I vowed then and there that I would never have gas in my house, and I haven't.

It was nearly always sunny in Tasmania and I remember seeing the front garden of Grandpa's house. It was high up a hill and the front sloped down towards the road. It was covered with flat stones and a lot of brightly coloured flowers on a succulent plant which I later learned was called Mesembryanthemum.

Mum and I were in the kitchen one day and another lady and a little girl came over from their house opposite. I was still as shy as ever and didn't especially want to have to meet new people. Mum introduced them, and I stood stock still and studied them without saying a word. Eventually the girl, who was called Jenny, spoke:

'When is your birthday?

I stared at her. She was about the same height as me, but she had brown hair and brown eyes. What a question, I thought.

'The eleventh of July,'

'How old are you?'

'Nine, so what?'

'That's my birthday too,' she said, 'and I'm nine too.'

'No!' Was she making it up? Her mum and she looked serious. It was really true. What a coincidence! I was intrigued.

I went across the road to her house and soon we were out at the back playing together as though we were twins and had been together all our lives. It was lovely to have a soulmate at last.

Chapter twenty-two

Photography

Jenny and I played together every day, sometimes at her house opposite Grandpa Seager's and sometimes in town.

Mum warned us: 'Don't go into St David's park late. It can be dangerous there.'

So we thought about it and decided that we must see this for ourselves. We arranged our secret visit. At five o'clock in the morning, or some dreadfully early hour like that when the sun was just coming up, I heard a slight scratching sound at my window. Jenny had come across to Grandpa Seager's and had thrown some pebbles onto the glass to wake me up in time.

I sleepily forced myself awake, got dressed and crept outside. We walked all the way along Sandy Bay Road towards the centre of town. The whole road, normally very busy with traffic during the day, was still asleep and the weatherboard houses were silently waking as they were touched lightly by the rising sun.

St David's Park was a small dark stretch of grass with gravestones stacked against the wall. It felt very creepy and it was easy to imagine the ghosts of dangerous people from the past dwelling in this strange place.

After a while, nothing dreadful happened, so we read all the tombstones and went home again.

Jenny was interested in photography. My Granddad Hammond had given me a fancy black camera and had taught me how to change the aperture and set the distance to take photos and I had become quite interested. But now my soulmate had taken this hobby to heart and was very heavily involved in taking photos and developing and fixing them herself, I wanted to do this as well.

We took a lot of photos and when the film was finished, we hid under the bed so that it was completely dark and carefully took it out of the back of the camera. We wound it inside a round plastic container called the developer. Once the lid was on, we came out into the light, poured the developing liquid into the container and swirled it round and round for some minutes. Finally, when we thought the film was fully developed, we lifted it out and cut it into a lot of separate negative pictures. When we lifted them up to the light, we could see the shapes of the people in the photograph, but they were black when they should have been white. We darkened the room, took one of the negatives, placed it on a piece of special photographic paper and put it under an orange light. Holding the paper with tongs, we put it into a tray of fixing liquid we had prepared and watched while the paper revealed the black and white photo we wanted. We did this to every negative in turn and put them aside to dry.

One holiday visit Jenny showed me how to put a glaze on our pictures. We spread talcum powder over a sheet of glass, put the photos on the glass face down and squeezed the liquid out of them with a rolling pin. We stood the glass up and as the photos dried, they dropped down, fully glazed.

I kept up this hobby for some years and even did it when I was in boarding school for a short while. However, after a few weeks one of the boarding house mistresses took me aside and said:

'Rosemary, we are pleased that you have taken an interest in photography, but I wonder if you could be a little more careful.'

'Oh?'

'Yes, the acid you use to fix the photos is making holes in our bath!'

Chapter twenty-three

Tennis

When I was about eleven years old, one of the afterschool activities Mum and Dad encouraged me to have was tennis lessons.

I rode my bike up to the tennis courts up on the hill of the town. The young man coaching us was slim, tanned and very good-looking so I enjoyed being taught by him. There were about a dozen of us lined up against the wire fencing of the tennis courts, all nervous, wearing shorts and sandshoes and holding our new or second-hand tennis rackets. The courts were orange-coloured and hard. We didn't have lawn courts in our town because the grass was always too dry in Australia. The sun was shining down on us gently. As this was the early evening, it had lost the harsh heat of the day.

We stood together in a higgledy-piggledy line, balancing our rackets lightly on our left hands. The coach went along our row checking that we were gripping the rackets correctly for a forehand. Our right-hand finger and thumb made a 'v' on the handle of the tennis racket. Then together, we stepped forward with our left foot while swinging the racket back as levelly as possible and swinging it forward imagining we were hitting the ball. We practised that a lot.

Next time we were shown how to turn our hand a little over to the left of the handle so that the' v' was no longer in line and we stepped forward with our right foot while swinging the racket back on our left side, swinging it forward to practise the backhand shot. This was more difficult that the forehand.

Later we learned to serve. We threw the ball up with our left hand, swung the racket behind us and then brought it up and over our head as we tried to hit the ball into the square of the tennis court on the other side.

After learning to volley (hit the ball when we were close to the net) we played a game of tennis, sometimes one against another and sometimes two against two when we could hit the ball into the tramlines on the outside of the court.

Near the end of the course we had a tennis competition. I was very shy in those days and was almost frightened to win. I was playing rather badly because of this until a young lad who was watching started egging me on.

'Go on!' he shouted, 'Hit it!'

I tried harder and was starting to win some points, but I was too late to win the match. I felt I had never had someone wanting me win to like that before and it cheered me up.

We were shown how to umpire and we practised being ball boys and girls like the ones that collect the tennis balls in important matches like Wimbledon.

Mum bought me a practice ball that was a tennis ball on a bit of elastic that was stuck in the ground. When I was at home and bored, I went out to practice and played with the ball for hours. I loved to feel the tennis ball when it hit the racket dead centre and seemed to speed away with little effort on my part.

I loved tennis and when I was at boarding school, I pleaded with the principal, Sister Jessica, to let me play in the tennis team.

Now, many years later, I love watching the tennis matches at Wimbledon and remember those sunny days practising on those tennis courts in Devonport.

Chapter twenty-four

Girl Guides

When I was eleven, I also had a special birthday treat. Wearing my Girl Guide uniform for the first time I stood before the leader of the Guides, held up my fingers in the Girl Guide salute and promised to do my duty to God and the Queen, and to help others at all times. I flew up from Brownies to become a Girl Guide.

Dad had shown me how to clean my leather shoes. At playtime at primary school I often took my own basketball. It was made of leather and every day I polished it with a brush dipped in a tin of brown polish. I brushed it all over the ball and then took a cloth and rubbed and rubbed until it was shiny and no bit of polish was left. I loved the smell of the leather. Having a leather belt to clean before Guides was nothing.

I was to be in the Galah troupe, so I had a Galah badge to sew on the arm of my uniform. A 'galah', as everyone knows, is a pink parrot and sometimes they can be trained to talk. Dad told the story that one afternoon he saw a parrot on the fence and said:

'Hello, you're a pretty parrot.'

The parrot replied: 'I'm no parrot, I'm a galah!'

Dad found this very funny and always said that this story was absolutely true.

At Guides, our leader was Miss Hill, a tall slim white-haired lady with a soft smile. She had also been my Geography teacher but that didn't matter; I liked her. She encouraged us all and we learned a number of skills we would never have learnt at school.

One evening we were all lined up for inspection to see that we were wearing our uniforms correctly when she walked up to me and stopped. I cringed.

'Look everyone' she cried. I cringed even further.

'Look at Rosemary's belt. It's so shiny, she must clean it thoroughly every time. That's right isn't it?'

I gulped and nodded.

Then she found out that I liked playing the piano and making up tunes. She asked me for a copy of one of my compositions. In those days you had to write every one out by hand. I carefully wrote out one of my first compositions in pencil and then went over the pencil marks in black ink until the whole composition was complete.

She was delighted to receive it and said she would save it for one day I might become a famous composer. Well you can't be right all the time, although I did keep composing a little, especially when I was a school music teacher and we had to put a little musical show on at the end of term. I wrote 'A Nativity Cantata': a number of very easy songs that told the story of the Nativity, how Jesus was born in Bethlehem and how the angels and the shepherds came.

Many years later at a meeting of teachers I showed them this composition saying how easy it was and that all we needed to do to encourage children to sing. Someone at the meeting asked if she might use my composition at her Sunday school. I was somewhat surprised but said yes. The following year she asked if she could use it again and asked if I would like to come along so that everyone could thank me as the composer. I felt very proud, agreed and made a note in my diary to be there. I drove to Soham, but I could not find the church nor any church hall open where my composition was being sung and played. After some time, I checked the details again and to my horror I had got it wrong. I had driven to Soham instead of Somersham which was miles away and I was far too late to be able to arrive even at the end of the production.

So much for my becoming a famous composer!

Chapter twenty-five

Camping

One of the most exciting things to do when you are a Girl Guide is to go on a camp. It was full of completely different chores to those I never did at home and I have fond memories of sitting round the camp fire singing 'Oh my lord how we roared in that old model Ford along the road to Gundagai, the radiator's hissing and half the engine's missing …'.

Just like Dad, Miss Hill was very careful to make sure we knew all about fire safety. We had to make sure we had cleared the area before we set up a fire. First, we put some stones down and then we added some very dry, very thin twigs, followed by slightly thicker ones until we had a pyramid with a little space where the air could get in and the match could light the fire.

When we finally got the fire going, we hung a billy can on a forked stick above the flames and made some dampers by mixing flour, salt and water, wrapping them round sticks and holding them over the fire too until they were cooked. When the fire died down, we cooked pudding on the hot stones. This consisted of bananas slit down the centre with chocolate stuffed inside.

The highlight for me was when we went hunting for witchetty grubs. We pulled the thick bark of trees that had fallen down and found the white wriggly creatures just underneath the bark.

One of the Guides said: 'You can eat it alive, you know. The aborigines did.'

I could tell by her voice that she was daring me to do it. I hesitated as I held the soft, plump little creature between my fingers. I wondered if it would still wriggle when I put it in my mouth before I bit it. Taking in a huge breath I opened my mouth and popped the little creature in and bit. It didn't wriggle. I know I had never had one of these grubs before, but somehow it tasted familiar.

We toasted them on the fire too. Years later someone reminded me what witchetty grubs taste like: they are just like marshmallow with peanut butter.

After the meal we had to make absolutely sure that the fire was well and truly out, and that no sparks could set the dry grass alight which could be a real danger in Tasmania.

I went on other camps. One was a church one and all I can remember of that was having to have stone-cold showers early in the morning. I wouldn't recommend it.

Chapter twenty-six

Doc Haward

By now I was in high school. I was in the second year of high school when I remember coming across Doc Haward. I was sitting at a wooden desk in the middle of the classroom when a lively teacher wearing a black academic gown swept into the room. From the moment he arrived we were transfixed. He spoke constantly in French, so we didn't know exactly what he was saying, but eventually, after giving us the words to use to give in an answer, we were able to reply to his questions.

His voice, his actions, his focus on each member of the class had us watching his every move. A few boys sometimes lost concentration, but Doc Haward was a good shot and a piece of chalk thrown in their direction soon made them pay attention.

Above all was the exciting feeling that I was automatically thinking in French without having to translate. It was amazing! He and the lessons were fascinating and I looked forward to his lessons every time.

Then Mum got to know him. Didn't she know everyone?

One day at the end of the lesson, while the rest of the class were still easing themselves out of the classroom, Doc Haward called out to me quite loudly, loud enough for everyone to hear:

'Your mother', he said looking at me directly. 'Thank her for her recipe for flummery. It is lovely but it makes gallons of the stuff. We've had it coming out of our ears!' He grinned.

My cheeks burned. He was only joking, I know, but I could have died with embarrassment.

Chapter twenty-seven

Mr Paterson

There was also a rather harmless English teacher who made a real impression on his class once. He was thin and old, too old for us to be especially interested in him, and he stood in front of the class, his rather worn suit hanging loosely round his skinny frame while he mildly attempted to teach us English. We largely ignored him, taking only an occasional interest so that he could claim to be teaching us and we could claim to be learning.

The one day, without warning, he suddenly started speaking not his own words but words that struck us immediately. We were given an insight into our Australian heritage, which made it so different to the English poems, stories and history that our whole curriculum was filled with.

He started reciting a poem: 'The Man from Snowy River'.

'There was movement at the station,' he said. We paused. This was different.

He continued: 'for the word had passed around

That the colt from old Regret had got away,

   And had joined the wild bush horses -- he was worth a thousand pound,

    So all the cracks had gathered to the fray.

   All the tried and noted riders from the stations near and far

    Had mustered at the homestead overnight,

   For the bushmen love hard riding where the wild bush horses are,

    And the stock-horse snuffs the battle with delight.

   There was Harrison, who made his pile when Pardon won the cup,

    The old man with his hair as white as snow;

   But few could ride beside him when his blood was fairly up --

    He would go wherever horse and man could go.

   And Clancy of the Overflow came down to lend a hand,

    No better horseman ever held the reins;

   For never horse could throw him while the saddle-girths would stand,

    He learnt to ride while droving on the plains.

And one was there, a stripling on a small and weedy beast,

  He was something like a racehorse undersized,

With a touch of Timor pony -- three parts thoroughbred at least --

  And such as are by mountain horsemen prized.

He was hard and tough and wiry -- just the sort that won't say die --

  There was courage in his quick impatient tread;

And he bore the badge of gameness in his bright and fiery eye,

  And the proud and lofty carriage of his head.

But still so slight and weedy, one would doubt his power to stay,

  And the old man said, 'That horse will never do

For a long and tiring gallop -- lad, you'd better stop away,

  Those hills are far too rough for such as you.'

So he waited sad and wistful -- only Clancy stood his friend --

  'I think we ought to let him come,' he said;

'I warrant he'll be with us when he's wanted at the end,

  For both his horse and he are mountain bred.

'He hails from Snowy River, up by Kosciusko's side,

  Where the hills are twice as steep and twice as rough,

Where a horse's hoofs strike firelight from the flint stones every stride,

  The man that holds his own is good enough.

And the Snowy River riders on the mountains make their home,

  Where the river runs those giant hills between;

I have seen full many horsemen since I first commenced to roam,

  But nowhere yet such horsemen have I seen.'

So he went -- they found the horses by the big mimosa clump --

  They raced away towards the mountain's brow,

And the old man gave his orders, 'Boys, go at them from the jump,

No use to try for fancy riding now.

And, Clancy, you must wheel them, try and wheel them to the right.

Ride boldly, lad, and never fear the spills,

For never yet was rider that could keep the mob in sight,

If once they gain the shelter of those hills.'

So Clancy rode to wheel them -- he was racing on the wing

Where the best and boldest riders take their place,

And he raced his stock-horse past them, and he made the ranges ring

With the stockwhip, as he met them face to face.

Then they halted for a moment, while he swung the dreaded lash,

But they saw their well-loved mountain full in view,

And they charged beneath the stockwhip with a sharp and sudden dash,

And off into the mountain scrub they flew.

Then fast the horsemen followed, where the gorges deep and black

Resounded to the thunder of their tread,

And the stockwhips woke the echoes, and they fiercely answered back

From cliffs and crags that beetled overhead.

And upward, ever upward, the wild horses held their way,

Where mountain ash and kurrajong grew wide;

And the old man muttered fiercely, 'We may bid the mob good day,

_NO_ man can hold them down the other side.'

When they reached the mountain's summit, even Clancy took a pull,

It well might make the boldest hold their breath,

The wild hop scrub grew thickly, and the hidden ground was full

Of wombat holes, and any slip was death.

But the man from Snowy River let the pony have his head,

And he swung his stockwhip round and gave a cheer,

And he raced him down the mountain like a torrent down its bed,
 While the others stood and watched in very fear.

He sent the flint stones flying, but the pony kept his feet,
 He cleared the fallen timber in his stride,
And the man from Snowy River never shifted in his seat --
 It was grand to see that mountain horseman ride.
Through the stringy barks and saplings, on the rough and broken ground,
 Down the hillside at a racing pace he went;
And he never drew the bridle till he landed safe and sound,
 At the bottom of that terrible descent.

He was right among the horses as they climbed the further hill,
 And the watchers on the mountain standing mute,
Saw him ply the stockwhip fiercely, he was right among them still,
 As he raced across the clearing in pursuit.
Then they lost him for a moment, where two mountain gullies met
 In the ranges, but a final glimpse reveals
On a dim and distant hillside the wild horses racing yet,
 With the man from Snowy River at their heels.

And he ran them single-handed till their sides were white with foam.
 He followed like a bloodhound on their track,
Till they halted cowed and beaten, then he turned their heads for home,
 And alone and unassisted brought them back.
But his hardy mountain pony he could scarcely raise a trot,
 He was blood from hip to shoulder from the spur;
But his pluck was still undaunted, and his courage fiery hot,
 For never yet was mountain horse a cur.

And down by Kosciusko, where the pine-clad ridges raise

  Their torn and rugged battlements on high,

Where the air is clear as crystal, and the white stars fairly blaze

  At midnight in the cold and frosty sky,

And where around the Overflow the reedbeds sweep and sway

  To the breezes, and the rolling plains are wide,

The man from Snowy River is a household word to-day,

  And the stockmen tell the story of his ride.

The class was silent. Mouths gaping, we stood still, amazed. How had he remembered all of that? Then one of us clapped and for once in his life, this English teacher was given a rousing cheer by his class. It is only now that I wonder if I have remembered his name correctly. For I thought his name was Mr Paterson, and the poem was called 'The Man from Snowy River' by the famous Australian poet 'Banjo Paterson'. I wonder now, were they related or had I remembered the name of the teacher incorrectly?

Then there was a German teacher whose name I forget. He had a huge egg-shaped head and he rode to our secondary school on a motor bike so that his helmet made his head look even larger. He too was a mild teacher, who chatted to us and occasionally made an effort to teach us. It was his teaching that told us how to pronounce the German 'ch'.

'You say "sh"' he said, 'and smile.'

Sure enough we got close to pronouncing 'ch' correctly even though it is a sound that is not in our language. He encouraged us to learn some German off by heart and I learned a couple of verses of a song that started 'Ich weiss nicht was soll es bedeuten ...' When I learned to sing many years later, the German I had learnt was useful. At least I knew how to pronounce some of the words without having to have the pronunciation explained.

A few years later, it was his class that I joined when I came back to Devonport from boarding school to sit with my old friends who were still at school while I was supposed to be on holiday. I sat among the class, he came in and chatted and didn't even see me (or he very wisely pretended not to see me.)

These were exciting times for in 1960 Yuri Gagarin was the first person to travel in space in a satellite. Dad and I often went outside at night to look at the star-covered sky. Devonport was only a small town in those days and we didn't have the light pollution we get now. The satellite could be clearly seen – a bright red light that swept from the right side of the sky right over and down to the left. It was fascinating to watch and I kept newspaper cuttings of the event.

I was still friends with Cora, but the competitiveness between us kept on going; it was part of the nature of our friendship. It finally got so bad that one day Mum told me Cora was a bad influence and I should stop seeing her. I knew inside that Mum was right and from then on I went to school alone. I felt very lonely.

After school I came home to an empty house for by this time Mum was working as the police magistrate's secretary. I ate too much of the cake she had left and grew fatter and fatter. I went for long walks along the seashore breathing in the fresh salty air trying to ease the ache of my loneliness.

After an art class at school one day, I had a special reason for going on my usual long walk to the Bluff.

Chapter twenty-eight

A walk to the Bluff

The Tasmanian sun was shining strongly as I swept out of the gate to my house in Devonport. Remembering to close the gate behind me, something I had learnt to do instinctively after my holidays on the farm, I took the path down towards the river. I shook off the cares of my busy school day and breathed in the fresh air tinged with eucalyptus and the sea. I glanced briefly at the shimmering leaves of the gum trees beside me as I walked. I would not stop to count the gum nuts today. I increased my pace, walking purposefully towards the river and onto the thin grass beneath the tall pine trees that lined the shore.

The Mersey River was full, its dark blue water sparkling. When I looked closely, the water swirled in different blues, some dark and motionless, others pale strong streams of a fast-flowing current. I would never dive into the water myself, no matter how hot it was. I knew it was too dangerous.

I paused for a moment at the junction where the paths met. I would not turn right and go into town; today I would turn left and follow the shore round to the Bluff.

No matter how many times I explored the shoreline, I would find something new.

The path suddenly narrowed. My foot trod on a tuft of hardened grass poking its head up from the thin layer of sand between tree roots that stood out on the path. I was glad that the blades of grass were not frequent or tall enough to cause me to worry about snakes. A thin line of black ants crossed my route. I stepped over it. At least there were no bull ants among them this time. I glanced ahead at the rocks.

I was coming closer to the rock pools. Quite often, I peered into the dark water and put my finger into the open mouths of the colourful anemones to make them spring their mouths closed. I would often see small fish wriggle beneath. They were plump little creatures, their shiny brown bodies squirming in the depths of the water. I wondered what kind of fish they would become. Perhaps they would slip out to sea when the tide came in and grow into the most common fish of all. I smiled as I remembered when I first asked what these fish with a flat head were called.

My brother had simply replied, 'Flat head, silly!'

I sometimes touched the little fish in the pools, stopping myself from recoiling from their slimy wriggling bodies.

By now, it was mid-afternoon, the sun was hard and bright, and I had something I must do. I crossed the path and stepped onto the large expanse of stony shore now well away from the river's edge. Not for me was the straight, boring path for I liked to stride across the stones with sweeping steps until I reached the larger rock pools. I would inspect the anemones, the crabs and the fish, and continue round the headland until I could see the beach at the Bluff. There my friends and I swam and played in the summer holidays when my family was not at their favourite beach down south.

My foot dislodged a loose stone which clattered down into a pool. I bent down and picked up a larger stone beside it. I would always be able to find crabs, but only once did I find a real whelk inside its shell. There was only one pale crab today. I replaced the stone carefully and pressed on.

I followed the shoreline, checking more rock pools until I came to a small sandy clearing. This was my beach, I had decided. I liked to imagine no one else came here. No one else sat for a moment in the strong sunlight, sitting and dreaming of the future, or just watching the waves roll in, pause as if taking a breath and roll out again like life itself: constant, never-changing and beyond anyone's control. When I sat on this tiny stretch of sand this time, I leant back, and listened to the faint hush of the boobyalla bushes and the gentle hissing of the sea spray. I let the glaring sun warm my face and decided to keep hold of this memory for the future, whatever that might hold. My destiny was a mystery that I would have to live through, over which I had little control and which was as inevitable as the next group of waves that struggled to shore.

Eventually, I stood, moving swiftly towards the path that I had decided to take, for I was impatient to reach my destination. I glanced briefly at the row of widely spaced houses that lined the road running parallel to the path, the white weatherboard shining bright in the glare of the sun in contrast to the darkness of the shade under the pine trees. I ignored the children's playground. I was too old for that now. The toy train looked silly and was only for little children, not for me.

I strode along the beach where my friends and I had played umpteen games of cricket during the summer holidays and then I turned up the narrow path and climbed towards the Bluff. I pushed my way through the thick boobyalla bushes that covered my route. I screwed up my nose at the strong smell of urine. It must have been left by some horrible people at night for I never saw them on the favourite walks that I went on nearly every day. I decided I wouldn't think any more about these nasty people who desecrated my sacred walk. As I broke free from the bush, I breathed deeply, my lungs welcoming the fresh sea-tinted air. The path was clear.

Finally, I came to some huge black rocks lying flat above a very deep cut. I tentatively stepped towards the railing protecting me from falling into the angry waves. I stood there for some time, peering carefully down at the frothing water below. I listened to the heavy boom of the giant waves as they whacked against the solid rock. The water sucked back with an enormous strength and thwacked again. Every swell and burst of spray was different. Sometimes the rocks roared like an invisible creature bellowing to free itself from its inescapable fortress; sometimes they only gurgled like a baby's first tentative explorations of the world of sound.

I eventually turned away from the giant rocks and walked quickly up to the look-out, its pale concrete steps and walls sitting high on the rocks like a rectangular nose on a ragged face. Although I was keen to make my new discovery, I couldn't break the ritual of my solitary walks by the sea; I had to go to the look-out. At the base of it, I read the plaque to a person who had died trying to save someone from the vicious waves. I shuddered. I was not afraid, but I couldn't help thinking how terrible it would be if I fell into those waters. I looked around. I was alone. There would be no one to rescue me if I fell. I peered down. I felt dizzy. I shook myself and stepped back. I turned and strode further round the headland, further than I usually walked for I was on my way to find my quarry.

I stopped on a stretch of flat brown stones that lined the path. I started searching the rocky shelf in front of more boobyalla bushes. There was nothing. I moved towards the bushes and moved them aside to see the rocks underneath. Then, at last, I found it! I recognised the shape. Carved on one of the stones was a circle, not a complete circle but one that had obviously been drawn by human hand. I knelt in front of it, running my finger round the smooth shape. I sat down and closed my eyes. I tried to imagine who had created this piece of primitive art, hundreds of years old. I slowly ran my fingers round and round it, and let my imagination run free. Into my thoughts came the image of a thin, semi-naked aborigine. His hair was curly and unwashed, his face a blue-black, the whites of his eyes in stark contrast to his features. He was humming a single note, a single continuous sound that was gravely and low. His long thin fingers held a stone in his hand which he held firmly down and pushed round and round on the flat stone before him. His thoughts drew threads of his life together as he dreamed of the ghosts that surrounded him. His mind was filled with pictures of speared fish drawn from the cold frothy sea, and of his loved ones taken by heavy storms, by fighting with the white strangers who had invaded their land or, slowly and painfully, by hunger or disease.

I smiled, my eyes closed, my freckled face absorbing the hot rays of the sun. I had found what I had been looking for.

Finally, I stood up and walked smartly home alone to do my homework, thinking about my find and the art teacher who had told us about this aboriginal carving. He was the same teacher who had once embarrassed me in front of the whole class. We had an art exam and we were supposed to draw something to illustrate what we wrote. I was going to draw an aborigine behind a salt bush but got it all wrong and the more I tried to rub it out the more smudged it was. I eventually gave up. The art teacher thought the effect was marvellous. I didn't let on that it had all been a mistake.

However, I did have one success with my short interest in art. One day I drew a picture of a cockatiel. We had one as a pet for a short while, but he just shrieked all the time so we had to give him away. I found out later that he would have been all right if he had had a mate. However, one day I painted a picture of him for an art competition for the Argonauts Club, a radio programme I listened to most nights after school. That one time, I won a prize and was sent a lovely book.

Chapter twenty-nine

Crystal sets and radios

Dad liked to try out various inventions and one of these was a crystal set for Peter and me. It was a box with copper wire wrapped round and round over a roll of cardboard and a crystal that touched it to give a crackling noise. We had to listen through an earphone and move a dial until the sound became clearer, and then we could hear our local radio station in Devonport. It was wonderful for I had never heard anything like it before.

When I was about ten, I went with a group of friends to the radio station in a main street of Devonport called Fenton Street. We were very excited because we had been told that some of us could speak on the radio. We lined up on the stairs and eventually it was my turn to read. I read the words on a piece of paper and I was told to stay behind. The others tried and were all told to go. I'd won it! I was chosen to read an advertisement live on the radio! I was thrilled. I ran home to Mum and as I knew she listened to the radio every afternoon, I asked:

'Did you hear me? Did you hear it?'

'What?'

'I was on the radio this afternoon.'

'Were you?' Mum busied herself at the kitchen sink. 'Sorry I missed it.'

Many years later after your granddad John, my husband, went into hospital with dementia, I wanted everyone to know how people who have this disease need help. I wrote a book called *John, Dementia and Me'* for everyone to read. It told the story of your granddad and me as we struggled with his illness. I wrote to the radio station and was invited to talk about the book on a programme.

My stomach was churning as we drove towards Cambridge and turned into the road that led to the radio station. By this time, I had stopped driving so I was being driven by a volunteer driver who eased the car into a parking space near the building marked 'Radio Cambridge', parking it perfectly first time. I liked the blue and light green colours on the building. It looked calm and friendly, although my feelings of unease increased.

I was desperate to be on time, so I had asked my volunteer driver to bring me there far too early. I arrived at the door and it wouldn't open. I waved to the receptionist inside and she released it. I went into the waiting room. There was one settee where you could watch TV, so, with a cup of hot coffee in my hands, I waited. My thoughts were getting more and more jumbled while I tried to think what I would say. It was a chat programme, so they might ask me anything.

When another person came into the room, I turned to look at him. He was a handsome, silver-haired man and we became so engrossed in our conversation that the person coming to collect us had to cough loudly before we realised it was our turn to go through the door that said 'No Entry' round the corridors and into the studio.

We were greeted by a smiling lady with long hair and a friendly manner called Sue. In a calm voice she described what would happen as we sat in our chairs, hands trembling, waiting for the show to start.

The man who was also taking part in the chat show was Terry Holloway, a pilot who told us all about his latest flight over New York. Sue was amazing. She had at least five screens in front of her that she had to manage while speaking to us. She had to keep track of news items and people's comments that kept coming in as well as making sure she gave regular updates on the traffic and the weather during our conversation.

I tried to pretend that I was at home in my sitting room, talking to a couple of friends, which was very difficult with huge headphones on your head, a microphone on a stick that you had to lean into so that you could be heard and a chair on wheels that had a mind of its own. You could easily slide away towards the back of the room if you weren't careful.

The conversation flowed smoothly until Sue asked if I would think of having a relationship with another person now that my husband was no longer with me. Without thinking, I said: 'No, because men my age only want a nurse and a housekeeper.'

When I'd finished having the chat and went outside to the car, Arthur was very tight-lipped. I'd forgotten that he had been listening to the programme. He obviously didn't like my comment about men his age. We remained friends though.

Chapter thirty

The cupboard in the hall

In many houses, the cupboard in the hall is a place to store the cleaning things: a mop and a bucket, a brush and various cleaning products and polish to keep the house spick and span. In our house in Tasmania these items were used not by Mum and certainly not by me, but by Mrs McGuire, a very kind cleaning lady.

Our cupboard in the hall in Devonport had three purposes. The first was to store the cleaning stuff and the second was a dark place where our cat could slink into a wooden box provided for her to have her kittens. Once you closed the door slightly behind you, you couldn't see a thing. It was completely dark and an in-the-cupboard kind of smell mixed with a lingering after-the-kittens-had-been-born aroma. I used to sit with our cat and she didn't seem to mind as one kitten after the other slipped onto the rags on the bottom of the slatted box. Luckily, she was a good mother for if there had been any difficulties I wouldn't have known what to do. She cleaned up each kitten in turn and I watched as the little wriggling bundles of wet fur searched for a nipple. I was fascinated by their tiny paws pushing into their mum's side, their eyes firmly closed as they latched onto a nipple and drank from her. Our cat regularly had up to six kittens and fortunately, Mum was a very popular person in the town so before she had finished nearly everyone I knew had taken, or had found someone to take, all of the kittens from us after about six weeks.

However, the main purpose for our cupboard in the hall was for Mum, not to store her things, but to creep into when she sensed there was a storm coming. She had an uncanny knack for knowing well before any of us, that a storm was about to descend on us, and pound and crack the air with thunder and lightning, smashing the cast iron roof with relentless rain for several hours until it had spent all its energy.

She was petrified of them. Dad had to leave work sometimes to come and rescue her. This seemed perfectly natural to me, for storms were frightening and I understood this kind of fear; I was scared rigid of other people's dogs and some residue of this fear remains with me today.

So when Mum was missing, all that needed to be said was that she was probably in the cupboard under the stairs. She was not alone. She was joined by the cat for the cat hated storms too. Mum also clutched another necessary item: a bottle of sherry to help her cope until the storm had passed.

Mum and the sherry bottle were good friends, and why not? In those days drinking alcohol was a natural thing to do in society; it didn't have the stigma that it has today. Every evening before dinner Mum and Dad would have a few sherries to relax before the meal. Sometimes the few sherries would turn into a few more and dinner would be a bit late, but that was part of the natural turn of events in our house. I used to feel really hungry and I become pale and upset waiting for dinner to be served.

Mum's popularity also meant that often there would be a perfect stranger from Scandinavia or somewhere exotic – a new friend Mum had made – at the kitchen table sharing the sherry bottle.

So whenever a storm brews, I think of Mum in the cupboard, waiting anxiously for it to pass. I heave a sigh of relief that she doesn't have to put up with storms any more and no longer has to suffer the anguish they caused her.

Chapter thirty-one

Mum and Dad's friends

Mum and Dad had a lot of friends. Nearly every day either someone was popping round to have a few drinks in the evening or we were going out to visit them. I remember the Sadlers with their lovely farm. They had three sons who were jokingly called Jack, Tack and Sack. They often went out hunting and the story goes that when they got up on a bright sunny morning, they would immediately say 'Let's go out and shoot something.' The two ideas don't seem to go together very well. We visited them often and once we went to sit by the little river that ran through their farm. The eldest son, John, had a fishing line and threw it in the river from time to time. He managed to catch a fresh trout for us to have which was lovely.

I'm not sure if it was on their farm or someone else's, but we often went blackberrying. The blackberries grew every year in a long patch that covered one of the fences to the paddocks. I would be given a bucket to fill while we all collected as many as we could. I hated getting pricked as I pushed my little fingers into the bushes trying to collect the little blackberries. However, Mum with her usual jollity and persuasiveness made me feel it was fun, so I looked forward to these blackberrying days.

It was on one of these trips that we found Snizzlefrits – a tiny baby rabbit that I tried, but failed, to keep as a pet, for our house was too cold. We brought home another black rabbit from such a trip. I kept him in a box at home, but when I looked at him he simply sat there looking miserable with his nose running. I was told he had myxomatosis, a disease spread among rabbits to make them ill so that they would stop eating so much of the farmers' crops. Sadly, as I had been warned, the rabbit died.

Then there were the Smales who had a beautiful camellia bush by their front door. Their daughter, Dorothy, and I kept in touch for some time and at one stage we thought we would explore the world together, starting with England, but as often happens with such plans, we never quite did this together.

There were also the Bonneys with their dairy farm and their shack at Hawley Beach where we sometimes used to have a holiday over the Christmas period.

Chapter thirty-two

A Tasmanian Christmas

Although it was in the middle of summer, we still had a traditional English Christmas. It was my job to decorate the tree on Christmas Eve. On Christmas morning, we would get up early and share out the Christmas presents from under the tree and then hang around until it was time to get dressed for lunch.

Christmas dinner was in the middle of the day. Sometimes it would be nearly 30 degrees and as I sat at the dinner table sweat poured down my face, but it was Christmas and I loved the way we celebrated it just like they did in the 'Old Country' (England).

Sometimes we would have a goose and I can remember it arriving live, so Dad had to chase it around the backyard, catch it and kill it with an axe. I tried not to think about this when the goose was served up with piles of vegetables for our Christmas lunch. We would finish with a hot Christmas pudding with sixpences cooked inside for us to find. Even though the room was bright with sunlight, Mum still poured brandy over the pudding and lit it so that the flames were just visible.

We often had Christmas at the seaside staying in Mr and Mrs Bonney's shack. Mr Bonney looked just like Clark Gable, a famous film actor at the time. Mrs Bonney was a slim, very lively lady who was always concerned that I should become more grown-up as I got older. When I returned to Tasmania grown-up and a teacher, she saw me in the car while she and her husband were collecting pine tree branches on the Parade that ran along the river. She rushed over and immediately declared she was thrilled to see I was grown-up now.

The friends that stood out for me, who were Mum and Dad's closest friends, were people they knew from their experiences in the war. These were the Bells. John Bell was Dad's best friend and once a year, very early in the morning, I would hear noises at my parents' window. John Bell would come and wake Dad at dawn for the Anzac Day parade. We often met the Bells out at Hawley Beach and I was very sad when I learned that one of his children had been killed on a yacht.

Then of course, there was a quaint doctor and his family who lived on the east side of the river, the other side to us. His name was Marcus Clarke and he was a very jovial short chap. We went to their place for breakfast once and I was impressed by his cooking skills. Instead of just sloshing around the eggs together to make an omelette Mum-style, he carefully whipped the yolks and whites separately. The omelettes were delicious. He amazed me when he admitted that he swam in the river. We had been told never to do that and sure enough, he described how he nearly panicked once when the current tried to drag him out to sea. He had had to swim in a zigzag fashion to pull himself out of the current and finally make it safely to the shore. He was lucky to be alive.

Chapter thirty-three

Mum making people feel at home

Besides these constant friends, Mum would quite often pick up waifs and strays and had the knack of making people feel at home, sitting them at the kitchen table to have a drink.

One evening Mum and Dad went to a Chamber of Commerce event. As a private, or as they called it a 'public', accountant Dad worked for himself so he was a member of the Chamber of Commerce – a group of business men who tried to make Devonport a successful place for people who worked. On this evening, the crew from a submarine that had berthed in the docks at Devonport were invited. Before long, Mum was chatting away to the captain. As they got to know each other better, the captain said to Mum:

'Do you know the best question to ask a submariner?'

'No,' Mum replied. 'What is it?'

The captain replied immediately: 'Ask him if he wants a bath.'

Mum quickly asked: 'Would you like a bath?'

'Yes!'

The next day, a friend and I were sunning ourselves on the veranda enjoying the peace and quiet, with the front door wide open for there was no one around. In the olden days we could trust our neighbours and we rarely locked our doors.

Suddenly, a taxi pulled up outside our house. We had no idea who Mum had met the night before, so we were very surprised when the door of the taxi was opened and a man quickly climbed out clutching a towel under his arm. He paid the taxi driver, swung open our gate, and dashed up the steps across the veranda and straight through the front door into our house.

I wondered if I should challenge him. I called out: 'MUUUM?'

Mum appeared and reassured us that this was a man she had met at the Chamber of Commerce meeting last night and that she had agreed he could come and have a bath in our bathroom. We went back to sunning ourselves on the veranda while listening to splashing noises coming from our bathroom.

Some other waifs and strays acquired by my parents were John and Betty Moore. I was intrigued by John's fingers which looked as if they had been squashed in some terrible accident. He was a farmer somewhere towards the centre of Tasmania and when Dad talked about John being in the war, a prisoner of war, too I think, I tried to imagine what a terrible time he must have had. Perhaps his fingers had been smashed when he was tortured. I'd never experienced anything bad like that, so it was really difficult to imagine.

Betty was beautiful, with fly-away hair and a very delicate soft complexion, and the décor of their house, with lovely flowery covers on their furniture, matched her complexion and personality perfectly. She suited John well for John seemed a nervous person, which I put down to his experiences in the war. Dad commented once that John was really worried about not having any money even though considering his assets, he was almost a millionaire.

Chapter thirty-four

Entertainment

Not only were Mum and Dad good at collecting friends, they often came up with amazing schemes and exciting events to fill the days. . We had no TV and we didn't sit down as a family to listen to the radio; rather we gathered at the kitchen table and Mum entertained us with jokey stories filling the house with laughter.

Once my parents decided we should go fishing. Dad had persuaded Mum that he needed a special car: a lovely old green Jaguar. I loved the smell of the real leather as I climbed into the back. We never had to wear seatbelts in those days. We went on journeys to see friends or occasionally we would go to Hagley to see Granddad and his wife, Aunty Ellie, who Mum told me wasn't my real grandmother – my real grandmother had died young giving birth to her youngest child, Uncle Gordon. I loved sitting in the car, apart from once when we drove towards Deloraine towards the centre of Tasmania where there was a long line of gum trees that made the sun flash intermittently into my eyes as the car sped past.

At other times we would visit Uncle Ted and Aunty Dorothy, Dad's sister, who also lived in Hagley, on a farm. They lived in a white weatherboard house like ours and we would join their four children for a meal. Uncle Ted was an elderly man with the bluest eyes I had ever seen and Aunty Dorothy was lovely. She was much more organised than Mum and when we were on our own in Devonport, Dad admitted that Aunty Dorothy used to organise him a lot when they were little. Dad later nicknamed her the 'colonel'. She organised the family to pay for a special window about Granddad in his church in Hagley.

Having such a grand Jaguar car didn't deter my parents from doing just what they wanted. So, on this day, they looked out the smelly old fishing net they had got from a sea fisherman. They put this smelly bundle into the boot of the Jag and drove us to Port Sorell.

Chapter thirty-five

Fishing with a proper fisherman's net

We arrived at the beach at dusk – just as the sun was about to set and as the night was slowly creeping in – the best time for fishing, when the fish come out to feed.

After a lot of commotion, Dad bundled the net up in its sack and carried it down to the beach. By now it was getting quite dark and hard to see everything clearly. We stood around in our swimsuits on the wet sand, deciding who was going to grab hold of the end of the net and drag it into the water. You and I would probably think the tallest person would be the best for the job, but no, the Aussie way was to choose the shortest – me. While I was interested in having a go, I wasn't necessarily that keen to take the lead, but as it was decided and who was I to argue?

The net was much heavier and rougher than I'd expected. I grabbed hold of the end, and pulled and pulled until the net was a little way over my shoulder. I trudged forward, my bare feet digging deep into the damp sand. The water felt cold when my toes first touched it, but as I waded further in and the water crept higher and higher, I gradually got used to it. As evening fell the sky became black except for the stars and a pale thin slither of moonlight, and the dark water began to sparkle. I was told later the sparkling came from tiny plankton in the water. It was very eerie. The only sounds I could hear were the soft murmuring voices of the people left on the shore and the slaps of the water on my body as I moved forward.

The sand beneath me felt flat and easy to walk on, but the water swelled around me and I was sure strange water creatures touched my legs as they slipped past. I couldn't bear think what they were and the water crept higher and higher. When it reached my neck, I felt my feet being lifted from the ground. I knew I needed to turn back towards the shore. I was alone in the dark with the star-speckled sky above and only a thin pale blanket of moonshine to guide me.

The net was quite light in the water and only when I reached closer to the shore and the net was out of the water did I feel its true weight. All the time someone had been holding one end of the net on the shore to stop it going into the sea completely; someone else came to join me at the other end as I struggled out of the water. Together we grabbed both ends and dragged the whole wet net across the sand until it was right out of the water and none of the fish could escape.

We examined our catch in torchlight. Along with lots of seaweed, there were some sea urchins and a few fish, including some flounder (a flat fish like plaice) and flathead, and one fish that looked quite menacing. It was a small round creature covered in prickles and puffed up into a ball. We ignored it for it wasn't edible. I wonder if not only should we have avoided eating it but perhaps we should have avoided it altogether when we were in the water. Just how poisonous were those prickles? We never worried about the dangers much in those days. Life was not worth living if you didn't take some kind of risk. Maybe this kind of attitude lost us our Prime Minister one year. Harold Holt used to go swimming and on day he was dragged right out to see by the current – he didn't survive like Dr Marcus Clarke, Dad's friend who swam in the river, did.

We took the fish to the water's edge and, by torchlight, degutted them by slitting them up the centre and clearing away the innards. We built a fire on the beach, put the fish in a frying pan to cook over a fire.

Delicious!

Chapter thirty-six

Food

Of course in those days we didn't have refrigerators to keep the fish to eat later. Mum used to preserve some things by putting them in salt. I can remember jars and jars of runner beans: each containing a layer of runner beans, a layer of salt above, followed by another layer of runner beans until the jar was full. We also had jars and jars of apricots cooked in syrup lining the larder at home. This was for our fruit in winter.

Sometimes we kept meat in a meat safe – a square box made of strong netting. It hung on a tree outside to let the air in and keep the meat safe from blowflies.

One day, we got an icebox. A man would regularly deliver a huge block of ice that was put in the top compartment and kept things inside the cupboard underneath cool until the ice had completely melted. Much later, when we got our first fridge, the ice box turned into Mum's filing cabinet and was filled with papers.

In the early days we didn't get milk in milk bottles; we had a can that we left on the veranda step and early in the morning I would hear the milkman rattle the can as he filled it with our fresh milk. The trouble is it didn't last forever. Mum used to warm it up until the fat from the milk formed a skin on top. This skin became our own clotted cream and I would sometimes have bread, jam and clotted cream for lunch. It was lovely, just as nice as the bread and dripping we had on other days. Dripping was the fat from the meat Mum roasted, cooled down and hard.

Mum used to complain that Dad always wanted three square meals a day. In the evenings we had meat and three vegetables (potatoes, carrots and silver beet from the garden) and a pudding. To keep Dad happy, Mum often cooked something for our midday meal too. I'm not sure if you would like what we had – but I liked it all. For our midday meals we would often have fricasseed brains, saveloys, macaroni cheese or black pudding, followed by bread, butter and jam.

In winter in Nicholls Street, we would have the fuel stove on all day so the kitchen was always warm and became our meeting place. Dad would put logs of wood on the fire to keep it going and every morning he would riddle it by moving a lever at the bottom backwards and forwards. This would bring all the bits and pieces left from the fire into the tray at the bottom which he would then empty. This left the fireplace clear so that the air could get into it and help the next fire burn.

We would stand in front of the stove to warm up. Mum would keep a large pot of barley soup on one of the rings and every evening she boiled it up and gave us a mug of clear soup. It was certainly warming, if nothing else.

Mum's way of cooking was to shove everything together as fast as possible and forget it. She was not a born housekeeper and I guess I've inherited this trait for I prefer to have a cleaner to do the housework. My brother is famous for complaining that the mashed potato was not lumpy like his Mum used to make it. He once got a slug in his salad that Mum had picked from the garden. He was very upset.

Although Mum made up her recipes quickly, some of them were quite tasty. I can see her now making egg custard by whisking up some egg yolks in a bowl with a fork, adding the sugar and milk and shoving the bowl in the oven.

One particular dish we call Ming Ling I still make and serve when I have my spa parties nowadays. One of my guests is William Evans who dined with royalty many years ago when he was Lord Mountbatten's aide. William simply adores the Ming Ling and gets upset if I present anything else, even roast lamb.

Chapter thirty-seven

Banana passion fruit

When I was a young girl in Tasmania I always got my own breakfast and when we were in Nicholls Street I could have leant out of the window and picked a white peach, but I only liked the yellow peaches. I quite liked one fruit in the garden and had it for breakfast every morning. It was long and pendant-shaped and grew from a vine that covered our shambolic garage. At first it appeared as a large pink flower, then it developed into a soft green fruit and eventually it ripened to become a yellow fruit, ready to pick. We called the fruit banana passion fruit. As passion fruit don't have a strong taste, I would pick some, squash their soft skins until the insides oozed out into my bowl, cover them with lots of sugar and milk and then eat them for breakfast. After I had been away from Tasmania for over thirty years I returned to see that same garage with its banana passion fruit and my first thought was that I was sick and tired of it. Logically I couldn't possibly feel like this so long, but I did, so I chose a different breakfast t.

When I was about eleven Mum started going to work and we waited for her to come home, knowing that as soon as she came onto the veranda step we would smell the fresh bread she had just bought from the bakery next door to the magistrate's court where she worked as a secretary. We didn't care that you weren't supposed to eat bread that had just been cooked; it was a real treat to watch the butter melt on it while it was still warm and we loved it.

Chapter thirty-eight

Mum at work

Mum really enjoyed her work as a secretary at the magistrate's court. She used shorthand and when she got phone calls at home she often wrote the messages down in shorthand, using short strokes and squiggles that I couldn't understand.

It was not long before Mum ran the office to her liking. She found, for example, that the policemen she made coffee for never stirred their cups and were always complaining that they didn't have enough sugar in them. Without turning a hair, Mum would blithely bring their coffee to them, and madly stir the cups in front of them before handing them over.

One day I had been on a long walk along the seashore when I saw a very strange man lift his coat up and point to his thingy. I thought him quite weird, gave him a wide berth and went on my way. In conversation with Mum, I innocently told her about this strange man and she went into overdrive.

'What did he look like?' she asked.

I shrugged my shoulders. 'He was just a man.'

'How old was he?'

'I dunno.'

'Well, what was he like?'

'All I can think of is that he looked a bit foreign.'

'Why?'

'I dunno, Mum. I didn't really want to look at him at all!'

The next thing I knew, Mum had gone to the police station and with the police tracked down the man and prosecuted him. It turns out he was bald and wore a beret – which is why he looked foreign. Only after I had been told this did I remember.

Mum's boss Mr Temple-Smith came from England and many people who came out to Tasmania from England were not liked because they complained that everything in England was much better that in Tasmania. They became known as 'Whingeing Poms' (Prisoners Of Mother England). However, Mr Temple-Smith didn't complain. He was not a Whingeing Pom. He became a friend of ours and, apparently, he was even accepted by the locals who decided he was such a good sport that he could be called a true Aussie.

Chapter thirty-nine

More friends of Mum's and Dad's

Dr Nowell was tall and handsome and I was in awe of him, as I was of his slim smiley wife who had a bubbly personality and entertained us all constantly.

Dr Nowell joined a group of Dad's friends playing golf. They used to joke that as he was the youngest of the group, they should leave everything to him.

One day Mum told us that Mrs Nowell had had a car accident. She had had a can of food rattling around on the back seat and when she had braked hard, it flew up and hit her on the head in the area of her brain that controlled her speaking. Now she could no longer talk. It was a real shame. When I next saw her, her personality was dampened, she was no longer bubbly and couldn't speak, which must have been very hard for Dr Nowell.

Mum used to get phone calls from her and I could tell by the silences and her replies that Mrs Nowell felt she could trust Mum to help her try to talk again. She finally learned to talk again even though the 'talking' part of her brain had been injured. Later when I was studying language development I remembered this and believed different parts of the brain could take over jobs that we used to think were the responsibility of only one specific part of the brain.

Chapter forty

Going to boarding school

I was quite happy at Devonport Secondary School. I had a lot of friends and we had a great time. I still kept in contact with my best friend in Hobart and we wrote to each other every week.

My friends and I at Devonport High School didn't take our studies too seriously. I remember once before a test saying to Mum 'Test me' thinking that was the only way to learn. Mum pointed out that it was no good testing me if I hadn't actually tried to learn anything. She may have saved the day, for from then on, I did make a bit of an effort to learn before our tests.

Mum still didn't like the riff raff that I was mixing with. I didn't mind – everyone was equal as far as I was concerned. However, Mum and Dad had always believed that if you wanted a decent education in Tasmania, you had to go to a private school.

One day, she asked me 'How would you like to go to another school? A boarding school in Hobart?'

I had no idea because I had never been to one. I shrugged my shoulders and said I'd give it a try.

There was a whole lot of fuss over buying and putting name tags on far more school clothes that I'd ever had before: hockey shoes, hockey stick, hockey skirt and blouse, several uniforms, white blouses and underwear along with PE uniform. This was certainly different from the shorts I used to wear at high school which only had a thin coloured stripe sewn on them to indicate your house.

Dad drove down to the school in Hobart in the Jaguar and I was nervous as it swept into the drive and pulled up in front of the columns of the front door of the school.

I was taken through the front entrance into the cool interior. Everything was dark, and the brown linoleum floor shone as though they used the same kind of machine that Mrs McGuire used on our floors at home.

I waited until Mum had stopped talking to one of the sisters. She looked just the same as the nuns in Roman Catholic Churches – all in black expect for a bit of white at the neck. She looked just like a penguin, I thought. This school was St Michael's Collegiate School where Mum used to go. After Mum had been talking for AGES she came over to me and said:

'Sister says you would make a lovely sister of the church.'

Not on your life, I thought but I didn't want to disappoint Mum so I kept it to myself.

I was shown into a dormitory and told which bed was mine. I dumped my case on it.
and looked around.

A small slim girl with freckles came up to me:

'What's your name?' she asked.

'Rosemary,' I replied.

'Mm,' she looked me up and down. 'I think I'll call you Lucy.'

'Why?' I asked

With a mischievous grin she said, 'Because you're loose in the head.'

I thought this strange for she hardly knew me but I thought nothing more of it. I had
little idea that this was going to begin one of the unhappiest times of my life.

Chapter forty-one

Being bullied

Nothing noticeable happened at first. I was accepted as a newcomer among the girls. One night, I was even included in a midnight feast. I was sound asleep in the cold dark dorm when someone was suddenly shaking me.

'Come on!' she whispered, 'Bring your stuff!'

I clutched the bar of chocolate I had hidden under my pillow as instructed and went to meet the others in a cupboard near our dormitory. When the door was closed we turned the light on. Still in our dressing gowns and slippers, the four of us sat in a tight circle, whispering in the excitement of our secret meeting. I didn't especially feel like eating a chocolate bar at that hour of night, but I went along with the game and slowly crunched my way through it. I was glad when we could all sneak back to bed. No one caught us. We got away with it – wow!

Then gradually the atmosphere changed. Before I could get to know anyone really well, I noticed they were keeping away from me. When I asked a question, they didn't answer. I was alone. Whenever I undressed to go to bed, I felt self-conscious, turning my back so no one could see me, going into all sorts of contortions so that no one could get a glimpse of my teenage body.

I longed for Mum's weekly letter that told me all about the neighbours and what she and Dad had been doing. The only other thing I had to look forward to was morning break when we could go to our lockers and get some food from the tuck boxes our parents had provided. Mum had made sure I had a full one, so every morning break I would eat all I could, for this was the only comfort I had.

When we were on our own, away from the prying eyes of the sisters or the teachers, the girls sneered at me, turning away from me and grabbing their noses as though I stank. They whispered to each other and stared at me, and still no one would speak.

One day I was having a bath when the chief bully swung the door open slowly, and then stood in the doorway staring at my naked body. I could have died. I knew there was nothing I could do but wait until she had tired of her little game.

I was no tittle-tattle. I told no one, I just put up with it for surely, some time, they would get tired of being so horrible, but they didn't. I went on doing all the jobs that I had to do and bided my time. One day school would end and I would no longer have to put up with this.

We were moved onto the veranda to sleep. There was only a thin wall and one pane of glass between us and the cold outside. In winter it was freezing and when you looked outside you could see the top of Mount Wellington covered in snow.

We were not allowed to have either hot water bottles or 'transitors' as Sister Jessica called ransistors, the little radios that ran on batteries. I made myself as comfortable as I could on the veranda in spite of the rules. I sneaked in a hot water bottle and I always took a big omnibus book to bed as if I was going to read it. I had carved out the centre of the book and put my illegal transistor inside, making sure the earpiece could not be seen as I listened to it and nibbled at an apple I had also smuggled in, so that I could eventually go to sleep happy. There was a little hot water in the evenings, but when I got up in the mornings there was none. I emptied my hot water bottle into the sink so that I could wash in water that was not actually freezing.

Otherwise I did my chores: I got up at 6.30, woke the girls for their piano practice, went into the hall on my own to do my own piano practice. I was glad of the relative peace. I crossed the school yard on the way and it was very cold and empty. I took my skipping rope and, in between playing, I skipped 200 skips to get myself fit for hockey and to try to get myself warm. It was very hard playing the piano with frozen fingers.

As the bullying continued, I threw myself into my books and my piano. They couldn't get me there for the teachers would have noticed. This is when I first decided to turn a disadvantage to an advantage. If I wasn't allowed any friends and no one would speak to me, I would use the time studying for I had nothing else to do.

Even my piano lessons were difficult to enjoy. The teacher would say, 'You'll never make it, so and so is much better than you.' I wrote home to Mum and Dad and complained. I missed my old teacher in Devonport. Soon afterwards I was sent to a better teacher as a private pupil out of school and I caught a bus to Sandy Bay where the teacher lived. Her name was Madame Helen George. I never did find out where she got this name from. It was lovely having a real teacher again who inspired me and put up with my 'funny little ways' and imperfect practising.

At the boarding school, another practice room was the dining room where an old brown piano sat in the corner. My so-called class mate boarders wouldn't dare bully me when I was playing there for it would be noticed. I could play my pieces for hours. One favourite I loved playing was 'Clair de Lune' by Debussy. I put all my feelings into my music. At least here I was free to express myself and I could create something without it being ruined. Well, that was until Stevie our gravelly voiced PE (Physical Education) teacher told me to be quiet so that she could use the phone next door.

The boarders joined the day girls for joint classes. I expected to have to sit alone as usual, but one day, to my delight, a day girl called Ros, who I had been friends with in Devonport, arrived at the school and came to sit with me. She later told me how thrilled she was to find a familiar face at her new school. She knew I was a little unhappy but had no idea that I was being bullied. She didn't know how grateful I was for those few hours of sanity we had together.

Ros has been a very good friend ever since even after she married her husband Mike. We've all kept in touch over the years. It's funny how your best friends for life are those you make at school.

After almost a year of this constant bullying, I decided enough was enough and wrote home to Mum and Dad asking if I really had to stay at this school. I explained what had been happening and was expecting them to quietly arrange for me to go home to school in Devonport. Not Mum. She and Dad came storming down to the school, had a long talk with the sisters and everything came out into the open. One of the sisters obviously felt miffed that Mum and Dad had criticised them and told me I should have 'stood on my high horse'. It was no good telling her that that would only have added fuel to the fire. I don't remember getting any apology, but I didn't care. I was glad it had been stopped.

I was given a room on my own and allowed to use Sister Jessica's bath. We were only allowed to wash our hair on certain nights and certainly not in between, but I washed my hair when I felt like it, making absolutely sure not a single hair was left in the bath after me.

My friend Jennifer and her family were one other reprieve from my awful time as a boarder. I would let them know when there was a weekend coming up when we could go home. Devonport was too far to try to go by train for a weekend, so rather than spend my time in an almost empty boarding house, I would spend the weekend with Jennifer and her family in Dynnyrne up on the hill near the reservoir in Hobart. It was heaven. We would talk and talk, and play illegal games of roulette behind closed curtains.

There were also days when Jennifer and I would meet after school and go into a special restaurant. We would go downstairs where no one could see us from the street and order banana splits. I loved the cream and ice cream – a real treat after the bland food we had at boarding school. Fort tea in the boarding house I just remember white bread and peanut butter.

Jennifer came to our banana split treats in her blue and white check uniform from Taroona High, her school (and the same school the Princess of Denmark used to go to), and I would be in my cream and burgundy-coloured uniform with my hat firmly wedged on my head. We would chatter about this and that, and I would bathe in the feeling that all was well, believing for a moment that I was the horrible person the other girls made out I was.

For my final year I stayed with Madame Helen George my piano teacher.

Chapter forty-two

Madame Helen George

She was very elderly, with a very wrinkled face and curled body but sparkling eyes that told me she was very much alive.

'See if you can play this, dear,' she said.

'That's lovely. Now do you think you can ...' she very gently made suggestions and it was fun to learn the piano again with a decent piano teacher.

However, it was a little different when I moved in with her as a lodger.

Her house was high on a hill. You had to go up steps to get to the front door and once you were in the hallway you had to make sure the door at the end was closed, for the house was shared with some foreigners I didn't know. Madame made little effort to be friends with them, so they remained strangers.

When I walked near the door at the end of the hallway, an enormous growl came through the door. It was their dog snarling. My heart stopped for a few beats while I fought my huge fear of dogs.

Once, when I was hanging the washing out at the back and just putting the final peg on my blouse, I heard an angry growl behind me. The dog had escaped! I froze.

'Help,' I called out meekly, hoping the people inside would hear me but also praying that I didn't annoy the dog by calling out too loudly.

'Come here!' a neighbour yelled to the dog. I didn't dare move until I heard their door shut. I waited for a moment, turned around slowly and heaved a sigh of relief. There was no dog.

My room was a tiny box room off Madame George's bedroom. I had a bed and a small desk. I had my radio for company, but otherwise we lived a quiet existence with me helping a bit – perhaps not as much as Madame George had planned.

We sat at the tea table in the sitting room in silence. I listened to Madame's jaw click as she chewed on her bread.

I once tried to start a conversation, 'We are thinking of starting a magazine at school.'

'That's nice dear. What are you going to call it?'

'That's the problem, I don't know. What do you think?'

Madame suggested a few good names. I thanked her, and we continued eating in silence. The magazine never got started.

Every morning I heard a gentle tap on my bedroom door.

'I've brought you a cup of tea, dear.'

'Thank you,' I murmured in my sleep. I really didn't want a cup of tea in bed. I hated tea and I didn't want to get up. I wanted to sleep in, but I had no choice. Piano practice time was early in the morning.

I dragged myself out of bed, changed into my horrid school uniform and walked slowly, still half asleep to the piano in the sitting room. Half-awake, I played through all my scales and pieces, and that was it. I was in no frame of mind to think clearly or to practise properly and Madame was at least kind enough not to interfere.

I left for school straight after breakfast, walked down the hill to Sandy Bay Road and caught the bus.

When I came home after school, I went straight to my box room and did my homework.

At tea time, Madame and I sat at the table and ate in silence again, except when she said occasionally 'Oh dear, I have to do the ironing.'

I knew that was my cue to say 'Don't worry, I'll do it', but I'm ashamed to say my tone of voice told her how unwilling I was and how I felt it was unfair that I had such a boring time when the other day girls had families who understood them and took them out to concerts and shows.

Only once did Madame George make a comment.

One day, after I had been particularly angry with my lot and so annoyed when she had asked me to do one more thing for her, that I had gone into my room and thrown my slipper at the wall.

When I came out for tea, she said:

'You know, Rosemary, do you think you have a chip on your shoulder?'

I wasn't sure what she meant, so I didn't reply.

As the months went by, it was obvious that she was a very elderly lady. Someone said she was already ninety years old.

What if she was ill? I would be the only person around to deal with it. I shuddered at the thought. I hated other people being ill. I was no nurse.

One evening at tea I asked:

'Do you think you should give me an emergency number I could call if you were ill?'

'No,' she replied, her jaw clicking louder than ever, 'It will be alright.'

Well it wasn't.

One morning I woke and looked at my travel clock. The cup of tea was late.

I struggled out of bed, put my dressing gown and tapped gently on Madame's bedroom door.

There was no reply.

'Madame?' I called. There was still no reply.

'Madame?' I called very loudly. I thought I heard a slight sound come from the room.

I slowly opened the door and saw Madame still in bed, her neck stretched out, her thin white hair strewn all over the pillow.

A rasping noise came from her throat. She could hardly breathe.

'Who can I call?' I asked.

She uttered a thin sound I could not understand. I leant towards her and waited.

'Phone book,' she managed to whisper. I looked around and saw her phone with the phone book next to it.

'Hotel,' she said and named a hotel.

'Who should I ask for?'

'Dr Jones,' she whispered and went straight to sleep. I looked at her frail body under the bedclothes and I could see it rise and fall gently. She was still breathing.

With trembling fingers, I picked up the huge black receiver on the phone, dialled the number and told Dr Jones that his patient was seriously ill, that I had to go to school and I would leave the front door unlocked.

I was cross with her. Why hadn't she given me this number when I'd asked? I left her, and with school bag under my arm, I dashed down the hill to catch the bus, praying that when I returned home she would be alright.

When I came back from school I found a message on the table saying that Madame George would be in hospital for a while.

I had to look after myself for a few days, but then, she got better and came home again. She was alright. It was as if nothing had happened.

Chapter forty-three

A different kind of birthday celebration

To this day there is one thing I have never forgotten about my stay at Madame George's and I have never forgiven her.

It was my birthday and Mum and Dad came down to take me out to a posh restaurant. I was really looking forward to seeing them, to going out so that I could relax, have a lovely meal at West Point and really feel spoilt. I would be able to chatter to Mum and Dad and tell them all my worries for they would understand.

I waited anxiously at the sitting room window. At last the familiar streamlined green Jaguar came into view and pulled up outside.

I ran down to meet Mum and Dad.

'I'm SO glad you've come,' I said giving them a hug. 'Shall we go?' I turned to get into the car.

'Just a minute,' Mum closed her car door. 'We should pop in to say hello to Madame George, first.'

I sighed and followed them to the front door, opening it for them to go inside.

Madame George was seated in her usual chair in the sitting room, a rug pulled over her knees.

'I am so pleased to see you,' she said as Mum and Dad leant down to shake her hand. 'I'm gather you're taking Rosemary out for her birthday tea.'

'Yes', said Mum, 'We are so grateful to you for having her. It's been wonderful. Thank you so much for what you've done for her with her piano playing.'

Madame smiled, her wrinkled face beaming with the praise. 'You know,' she leant forward, stretching her scrawny arm towards them, 'I could make you tea here if you liked. I could do some scrambled eggs.'

I glared at my parents. They wouldn't dare, would they?

'Why, that would be lovely' said Mum. Dad, the traitor, nodded in agreement.

WHAT? I screamed inside. The last thing I wanted to do for my birthday was to have another meal of scrambled eggs with Madame! I seethed through the meal and just managed to stop myself from smashing the plates when I did the washing-up.

That was one birthday I have never forgotten!

However, there was one good thing about living with Madame George. I had turned seventeen and could have driving lessons.

'There's man who lives across the road,' Madame George said. 'He teaches driving. He's just lost his wife to cancer and I'm sure he would like the diversion.'

I climbed into his huge car and he carefully guided me through what all the pedals and levers did. I'd already had a go at driving at home.

Once my brother said he would take me for a test drive. Within five minutes we were arguing, brother-and-sister-style.

Peter leapt out of the car. I sat at the wheel and fumed.

'I'm never teaching her to drive again!' Peter snarled at Mum when he went in.

'I'm never getting in the car with him again either!' I shouted as I stomped to my room.

However, back in Hobart my teacher was much more patient and I must admit I was more willing to listen to his advice.

'See the edge of the window in your mirror,' he said as I was trying to park.

'Line that up with the pavement and carefully ease the car back.'

After a number of goes, I did it!

The day of my driving test came.

In those days there was not a lot of traffic in Hobart so getting your driver's licence was much easier than it is in England now. I didn't even have to sit a written test.

With my teacher at my side, I pulled up at the police station. I was expecting an examiner, a man with a clipboard, to climb into the back seat.

Instead a burly policeman, his shiny buttons straining to cover his dark blue serge stomach climbed into the back seat.

'Drive straight forward and turn right,' he said. I was going to be tested by a policeman!

He continued to give me directions and I drove very carefully, checking my mirror often and looking behind me before I turned a corner.

Then he said: 'Just park her in front of the bank will you? I need to pop in.'

'Pardon?' I blustered. 'But there are yellow lines there! I'm not supposed to park on double yellow lines!'

'Ah, no worries. You'll be fine,' he said.

Now I was in trouble. If I followed his advice and parked on the double yellow lines, he could fail me in my test and I could be fined. If I didn't do as he said, he could also fail me. I couldn't win.

I took a deep breath and parked, my heart thumping while I waited. What if another policeman came by and fined me? My policeman took ages popping into the bank and coming out again.

Finally, his plump figure rolled to the car.

My heart was on standstill when I pulled up at the police station and waited for the verdict.

'You have passed,' he said, leaving the paperwork with my teacher and dashing into the police station.

I was looking forward to driving Mum's car when I went back home to Devonport.

Chapter forty-four

A new home

I was at boarding school when I received amazing news. 'We are moving to 3 Nicholls Street' Mum's letter said.

I could hardly believe our luck. I had admired this large rambling house with its romantic attics and large garden for a long time. Our Business Principles teacher at high school had lived there and just as he drew completely straight lines for his business pages on the black board, the house and garden were in perfect order, all the flowers in a row as if they were standing to attention.

We had lived for so long in those two flats made into one house on Victoria Parade. My room had been cold and the curtains mouldy, so I wouldn't miss it.

I picture the time I spotted the teacher in the garden and noticed how the sun blessed the whole house and garden much more than it did our place on Victoria Parade.

I was glad I wasn't able to go straight away to the new house. In Mum's letter she moaned that she had no stove to cook on. She had to use a portable gas one that we used when camping. I had no idea how she would juggle all her saucepans on such a small space.

'I bags the attic rooms!' I said swiftly as our family gathered to make important decisions.

'I want them!' Peter said.

'You can have the room downstairs, it's much larger,' said Mum to him.

I was thrilled when my parents persuaded my brother to let me have the attic rooms.

I could see me in the future, a famous composer sitting at my desk overlooking the garden, making up world-famous melodies or writing pages of poetry that people were clamouring for.

I dashed upstairs and ran to the attic window. I leant on the sill and stared dreamily at the huge oak tree and Mum's vegetable garden. Dad's car was in the garage with the vine trailing over the garage in full leaf.

There was another attic room at the front. I dashed across to this room and sat on the seat at the window absorbing the hot sun as I admired the gum trees lining Nicholls Street. I leant forward and looked down the road. Yes, I could see elderly pine trees leaning forwards and framing a small blue patch of the Mersey River.

This was going to be wonderful!

Chapter forty-five

Bees

We soon settled into our familiar life style. Mrs McGuire came to do the cleaning and I would hear the polishing machine buffing the bare floorboards of the sitting room. It felt as though we were the remnants of a well-to-do family settled in a new land, in a large house that suggested wealth, grace and good living.

Unfortunately, as the years went by, somehow it was never quite maintained that well. While there was a magnificent fireplace in the sitting room, when we sat in the armchairs to enjoy the heat from the roaring log fire Dad had made, their centres sank and their arms cried out for a little care.

While my piano sat grandly next to the wall in the sitting room and my playing echoed through the house as though from a forgotten time, the wallpaper desperately needed changing.

The dining room looked grand with its chest of drawers and large dining table, but the strip of carpet underneath told another story. It was threadbare, but we didn't mind. We loved rattling around in this spacious new home.

Dad started getting involved in a string of hobbies.

One year, he decided he would have some bees.

'Wouldn't it be lovely eating our own honey?' he said.

'Yes,' I said, 'but bees sting. How are you going to get the honey without being stung?'

'Oh, it'll be alright. I have all the gear you need, and all you need to do is to push smoke into the beehive to make the bees drowsy and drop to the bottom. Then you can get out the honey from the sheets of wax that they have made. You'll see; you'll love it!'

Within a few days, a white beehive was sitting in our garden.

I still didn't think it was a good idea and wondered who would be the first to be stung? Me. I was bringing in the washing from a long line drawn across the back yard. I grabbed a sheet, not realising a bee was sitting on it and, naturally, he stung me hard on my finger.

'Ow!' I yelled. It really hurt.

Mum dashed outside and brought a 'blue' bag from the wash room.

'Here,' she said, 'put this on it.'

I held the little bag firmly on my finger and stomped inside, leaving the washing to fall on the ground.

My finger swelled and throbbed for ages although I had to admit that the blue bag helped to ease some of the pain. My finger remained swollen for days.

The 'blue bag' was normally used in the olden days to contain a tablet of blue that was put in the white wash to bring out the whiteness of the sheets and shirts.

Now we had a beehive in the back yard. Dad dressed up in all the fancy gear and put his 'smoker' at the entrance of the hive and waited. When he thought no bees were left working at the top, he carefully lifted off the lid, pulled up one of the trays holding the wax and honey, and took it into the kitchen. There we drained out the honey and put it into bottles.

Soon a neighbour leant over our fence.

'How's the beehive?' he asked.

'It's fine,' Dad replied.

'You know,' the neighbour peered round the side of the house, 'your bees have been getting a lot of nectar from my flowers.'

Dad got the hint and soon all the neighbours were given a free jar of honey.

The fresh honey was delicious on bread and butter.

Dad read up on how to keep bees and discovered that he was supposed to go deep into the hive, take out the queen bee and take the lice off her.

'Well!' he said, 'I'm not going to do that! They must think I'm mad!'

Eventually the bees got a virus and died, so that was the end of this hobby.

Chapter forty-six

Getting to university

Which university I went to depended on my A level grades. Dad had made me stay an extra year at school, so I was able to do some extra A levels that would help my score.

Music was my main interest for I loved playing the piano on my own, but I was also expected to play for other people. I had to play in assemblies taking my turn along with Penny Salmon and others.

At the beginning assembly the girls at the school stood in rows in the hall and while Sister Jessica was walking up the steps onto the stage we sang a hymn. Many of us stifled our giggles when we sang 'hobgoblins and foul fiends' in one of the hymns just as Sister Jessica made her way up the steps. Still trying to keep a straight face, I played Sister Jessica a note and she intoned some religious words. I never enjoyed playing in public like this, but realised it was just one of my duties along with the other ones I had to do as a boarder.

As a day girl at school I wasn't so affected by the nastiness of the boarders. However, Madame Helen George was well into her nineties and so not the ideal companion for a sixteen-year-old.

Fortunately, the Burleys, who were friends of Mum's, lived within walking distance. Every time I felt fed up, I walked along the road to their Sandy Bay house. They were a lovely family. Mrs Burley was very friendly and welcomed me whenever I appeared at their door. I was soon sitting at their dining table chatting with their younger children and talking about their older sister Victoria who I envied a lot because of her tremendous musical talent. I mentioned one day how difficult it was to study at Madame George's because I only had a tiny table in my little box room that adjoined her bedroom. Before I knew it, I was given a huge desk in the Burley's front room where I was able to devour books on Ancient History and study to my heart's content.

The day of my Grade 8 piano exam came. It felt strange being examined in the room where I was taught by Madame George and where I practised every morning.

Mr Farren Price had come all the way from Melbourne to Hobart to examine me and some other pupils from Hobart.

I was very nervous and as the exam progressed, nothing went right. I stumbled over the scales, stopped several times in the first two pieces and by the time we got to the last piece, I had given up all hope. I had failed the exam. I threw myself into the piece and enjoyed it for its own sake, as after all, nothing mattered now. Furious with myself, I just managed to answer the final exam questions and without a word, I stormed out of the room, flung open the front door and rushed off down the hill. I walked for ages until I had calmed down.

I didn't want to know the results when they came, but to my amazement I was given honours! Wow! The examiner said he had seen my potential in the last piece.

I had learnt one of Debussy's Arabesques and Madame George sent me to the studio of the ABC radio station to record it. Some of her other pupils had played on the radio many times before. When I arrived I was sent into a room and left there. I couldn't see anyone to talk to, so I talked to myself a bit, shrugged my shoulders and began to play. I messed the piece up a little but finally ended with a flourish. I was let out of the room but no one said anything and I was never contacted by the radio station again.

School eventually ended. A lot of the girls were tearful and sad that their school days were at an end. Me, I couldn't care less. At last, I thought, I was free.

I went home for the holidays to await my A level results.

The day came and the A level results were announced the *Mercury*, the newspaper produced in the Hobart. I wandered down from my attic room at the usual time still in my dressing gown to find Mum and Dad sitting anxiously willing me to open the paper to find out my results. I casually searched the newspaper, saw my results and murmured, 'Yeah, they'll do.' Then I went to get breakfast.

Mum and Dad grabbed the newspaper were thrilled. Three honours for Music, Ancient History and Biology plus a pass at French and English as well as a few O levels helped me to get a scholarship.

I was invited to the education offices in Hobart to be interviewed for a special scholarship overseas in Melbourne. 'As long as I didn't have to play the piano,' I thought. I brushed up my school uniform with its horrible burgundy and cream colours that have never suited me and arrived at the office. I was ushered in by a rather dishevelled chap who chatted to me about what I could do. His fingers were stained yellow with nicotine. As I watched him he put a cigarette in his mouth with the filter the wrong way round. I forgot to listen as I stared at the cigarette waiting to see if the man would light it or manage to turn it round first. I said 'yes' to everything.

'Oh yes,' he gushed enthusiastically, 'you could come back to Tasmania and do a recital in Hobart Town Hall,'

'I'd be delighted to,' I lied, thinking underneath it would be the last thing I'd want to do.

I returned home to wait and see if I had won the scholarship to a place at a college in Melbourne or whether I would be going to Hobart Uni. At the last minute, it was to be Melbourne!

Mum was so excited she rang the newspaper, and someone came round from the Devonport *Advocate* and took my photo with me clutching my music case that was too small to hold my music properly, and wearing a very expensive suit I had been persuaded to buy by a zealous saleswoman in Hobart. I was in the paper.

Chapter forty-seven

Water skiing

Have you ever felt that nothing goes right for you? When I was young, there were a lot of times when I messed things up. Fortunately, everyone was very kind about them, which made me feel even worse.

In my teens, Mum decided I really ought to go out and meet people. She sent my brother and I to have water-skiing lessons. I stood in my swim-suit and life jacket on the pebbled beach, with my feet in the skis and my hands holding the ropes tight and I listened carefully to the instructions. The speed boat was going to pull me up onto my skis and I would ride on the water. The speed boat revved, I bent my knees and gripped hard. The boat pulled out swiftly, I went forward, but, alas, went head first straight into the water. We tried again and again, and I thought I would never get the hang of it.

My brother, of course, grabbed the ropes and without bending his knees much or following any of the other instructions, he got up first time and went whizzing across the water as though he had been doing it all his life. Brothers can be so annoying sometimes.

Eventually I got the hang of water-skiing and really enjoyed the feeling of the salty breeze rushing past my face and the exhilaration of skimming across the top of the water, mastering the tiny bumps over the tiny wakes the speedboat formed.

When our next-door neighbours, the Hebblethwaites, invited me to come with them and do some water skiing I grabbed at the chance. We drove to a creek further inland called Horsehead Creek, because it was in the shape of a horse's head. Swimsuits, life jackets and skis were at the ready.

We clambered out of the car and they got the boat off the trailer and struggled with it to get it into the water. Then one of them got into the boat and tried to start the engine. It wouldn't start. This skiing session looked as though it wasn't going to be as exciting as the experience I had before. After trying again and again, they finally got the boat going. However, they then found that the steering had gone.

'Rosemary,' the driver shouted back to me.

'You'll have to help.'

I held my hands out: 'How?'

'Lean over the back of the boat and see the rudder thing that steers the boat? Hold that steady, will you?'

Tasmania is just about the nearest place to Antarctica and the water is freezing, absolutely freezing. There I was, bottom in the air, arm freezing in the water while I held onto the wretched rudder. My hand was positively blue when I finally lifted it out of the water.

At least this time it wasn't my fault and I was used to things not going well, so I just sighed and put up with it, vowing not to accept the next invitation to ski with the Hebblethwaites so quickly.

Chapter forty-eight

First year at university

Before I went to college I spent some time staying with Mum's sister, Aunty Joyce in South Yarra in Melbourne. I had been there on holiday before. In summer it was so hot that the pavement melted, and as you stepped forward your feet sunk into the bitumen leaving holes where your feet had been. The sun was so strong it bored into your eyes reflecting angrily off the white walls. When I went to the beach, I sat in the sea, an umbrella shielding me from the harsh sun's rays and I was still too hot.

Eventually I went to the college where I was to stay. Janet Clarke Hall looked like the university buildings in Cambridge and Oxford I had seen in pictures. It was a tall imposing building made of brick with large bow windows overlooking a narrow path.

I was shown into a large room with two beds. I would be sharing, something I wasn't used to. The carpet was very old. I'm not sure what colour it was supposed to be – it might have been blue once. There was a large table at the window. 'It would be nice to work there,' I thought and wondered who my roommate would be.

'Hello, I'm Janet,' a cheery voice said behind me. I turned to see a slim, dolled-up young lady who was far too sophisticated for me.

She continued, 'I'm going to be your roommate. Which bed would you like?'

I'd already dumped my case on the bed by the window. 'This one?' I asked shyly.

'That's fine. I'll take the other one,' she said and she started unpacking her case.

Janet and I got on as well as you might expect having completely different personalities. Janet was slim, outgoing and took great care to get her make-up on just right whereas I was plump, shy and hardly wore any make-up at all.

We settled into our different timetables, me doing Music and Janet doing an arts degree in Geography.

One day, I couldn't believe it. She shot out of bed, saying 'I'm late for the field trip!' .

I expected her to grab her bags and run out of the door. But no, she still carefully put on all her make-up first. I was amazed she got there on time.

Most universities have a rag week when the students get into mischief. Being a new girl, I decided to join in. One of the pop singers of the day was PJ Proby who was known for moving his pelvis in a sexy way (like Elvis). Three of us decided to dress up as fans, wearing ghastly colours that didn't match. I wore pink and purple. First, we decided to have lunch at our usual rather posh restaurant in Carlton, a place near the university. After that, we tried to hail a taxi. So many of them ignored us not trusting these three outrageously dressed girls. We finally got to the pretend show, and threw ourselves about like demented fans. I had a lecture to go to soon afterwards so I didn't bother going back to my room to change. When I sat next to my closest friend, he didn't recognise me!

There was another time when I had difficulty getting a taxi. I'd gone to St Kilda on my own to see an opera. I wore my suit and stood outside the theatre trying to hail a taxi. Every time I lifted my hand a man who was obviously not a taxi driver, slowly drew his car up to me. I waved my hands saying 'no, I really did want a proper taxi.' I found out later that not only was St Kilda the place to go to see operas in the theatre, but it was also a place where prostitutes hang out.

In my first year at college I noticed that everyone seemed that much more grown-up than me and I finally made a decision. I needed to lose weight. It was easy to do that in college when all I had to do was cut down on eating. I ate just a salad and an apple a day and coffee. I lost a lot of weight but had no idea that I had gone too far and become what we call these days 'anorexic'. In my heart of hearts I knew something was wrong but I ignored it. I was feeling more confident now and that was all that mattered.

I went on a trip to the university in Perth in Western Australia with the university choir. It was great. We sang 'Carmina Burana' and I set my eye on a rather handsome Russian student. I can still see him now up on the balcony singing his heart out with the rest of the men and booming out intoxicating chants.

Mum and Dad came to visit me in college and Mum panicked when she saw how much weight I had lost. I told her it was deliberate, and I was fine. Dad said later that he could hardly persuade her to come away, she was so worried.

Eventually the holidays came and I went home. Mum plied me with questions including 'Are you pregnant?' 'No,' I replied. 'Here, have some gin,' she said, immediately plying me with drink, trying to save her little girl.

After a lot of fuss, I went to the doctor on campus when I went back to college. He only suggested I was fat – probably because he felt the muscle I had built up with all the exercises I had been doing. However, that visit was enough for me to decide there must be something wrong and I started eating sensibly.

We were very poor at university. It was a matter of pride how we lived on our meagre pocket money. I walked wherever I could to save on the tram fares.

When I was in the second year of university I had a room to myself. It wasn't very cheerful although it did have an open fireplace. I was allowed to redecorate so I painted the walls white and made my own bedspread of blue linen.

I walked into town and searched for a picture to cheer me up. I missed my walks by the sea. I looked in the window of a shop that sold paintings and there it was, a large print showing frothy waves breaking gently on a deep blue sea, just like the waves that I used to stare at for hours in Devonport. I had to have it! I rushed into the shop and bought it.

How was I going to get it back to college? The usual way, I decided, and holding this rather large picture awkwardly in my arms, I struggled all the way a mile or so back to college and put it on the wall.

After this trip it finally dawned on me that all this walking ended up costing more than the tram fares would because I had to keep buying new shoes!

It could get very cold in Melbourne. Sometimes the icy wind cut right through you. I was so glad I had a fireplace in my room. The college had a supply of logs so quite often I would collect the wood, put newspaper, kindling and logs in the fireplace and light the fire. I loved to watch the flames as they grew higher and higher. I breathed in the smell of the wood and remembered those days in Devonport when I sat with Mum, Dad and my brother round the roaring log fire Dad made every Sunday night.

Then I would sit over the warm fire in my room in college, my feet on the mantelpiece and listening to a record of Mendelssohn's violin concerto.

As the sounds of the violin filled the room, I closed my eyes and let the music flow. It was if the violin was sweeping up all my feelings and holding them for me. All the sadness and pain I had ever felt was in the music and I let myself dwell on everything I had stopped myself from feeling. Sometimes my eyes would fill with tears, but I was alone, so nobody could see. It was a special time when I understood how lucky I was to be able to spend my days with something that I truly loved – music. It was bliss.

Chapter forty-nine

David

One of my closest friends was David, a dark-haired, wonderful pianist with a joyful smile and a lovely, rich voice. He and I got on very well and sat at lectures together. He would often pop into college for a coffee with me and my friend Helen who was training to be a vet, and we would have a great time.

I joked about things that went wrong. One time I described how I was asked to play the piano for a class to show how one of Beethoven's sonatas started. The lecturer was so impressed that he asked me to play it again. The second time I played it, it was AWFUL, and I even played a bum note. David sat on the bed, one leg balanced on the knee of the other and his head tilted. His friendly face broke into a huge smile and he giggled with delight.

One time he came in the morning after I had called a lecturer's bluff and had spent the whole night finishing some orchestration. This had meant carefully adding tiny notes for every instrument in the orchestra to a large page of over 200 lines. It took ages. It was no wonder I was feeling a little out of sorts when David came over for his usual morning coffee. He was lucky to get any as the hot kettle wobbled dangerously in my hands.

Then, it suddenly dawned on us —no gentlemen were allowed in the college until after lunch. David was there illegally.

'Quick,' I said, 'You have to go!' We laughed as he hastily slunk out of college, hoping he didn't meeting anyone on the way.

When I was in my final year my teacher entered me into a concerto competition. It was very like the piano concerto competition in the film *Shine* set in Australia. David was entered into the same competition.

With a concerto you needed to have a second pianist, so I asked David.

I practised and practised the last two movements of the Schumann piano concerto where many times, the pianist had to play up and down the piano at great speed. Getting every note mattered, so I practised again and again making sure my fingers hit every note exactly. When I was fully up to speed, my fingers raced across the keyboard automatically. In the performance, I felt as if I was watching someone else playing with a real orchestra. I filled the music with my feelings and my fingers sped up and down, changing the mood suddenly, pausing for a moment to express real sorrow or suddenly jumping with joy.

Even David commented, 'You're like a real virtuoso, Roe.' He was very talented himself. He could sight-read the second piano part to my concerto easily. When I played this concerto with David at the second piano during my lesson, Mr Farren Price was amazed at his talent. After he had teased us about what we got up to when we weren't practising, he asked David who taught him. I wanted to say, 'Leave him alone. This is MY lesson!'

We didn't get up to anything when we weren't practising, sadly, but David and I are still friends.

Chapter fifty

Learning how to socialise

Back to the time when I was first in Janet Clarke Hall at Melbourne University, I was still shy when it came to going to parties and meeting other boys. A student called Jane helped me. She had long wavy blonde hair, facial features fit for a fashion magazine and a slim and elegant body. I envied her, yet I knew that she too, was shy.

'You know,' said Jane, 'I've always been shy.'

I stared at her.

'You have?' I asked.

'Yes. Would you like to know how I cope? When you go to a party or a dance, stand out alone so that the boys can see you are not with someone.'

I grimaced – I was already a wallflower or 'wallweed'. If I stood out alone, no one would come.

'Try it,' she smiled. 'And when you meet someone, tell them how you are shy and that you don't like parties and dances. Be yourself.'

'Mm. I'll think about it.'

'And try these moves when you are dancing.' She stood up and swayed, moving her hips and her arms in an easy gesture again and again. I copied it and there we had it. I'd always found it difficult trying to dance the modern way with no set steps, that was so unlike the waltz we did in dancing classes when I was at school.

When I was at the boarding school, once a week we went to dancing classes with the boys from Hutchings, our partner school. An old gentleman played 'Tea for Two' on the piano and we ungainly teenagers struggled with our personal embarrassment and our clumsy feet trying to dance the quick step, the waltz and the cha cha cha. I never did master them.

Now at discos we abandoned these formal dances and did our own thing, which I found even harder. I decided to try out Jane's advice and it certainly helped.

Chapter fifty-one

Wog

One year, I arrived home to Nicholls Street for a well-earned rest after a difficult time at university and I was greeted by an ugly ball of wiry brown fur. It jumped up at me again and again, its long black claws making scratches on my legs.

'Don't do that!' I snarled at him, but he took no notice and placed another ugly scratch on my plump leg. At least he hadn't drawn blood so I didn't have to go and have a tetanus jab. However, I know from that moment on, he and I were not going to be friends.

'He's a stray that just happened to attach himself to us,' Mum explained.

'What's its name?' I asked sullenly as I pushed him down again.

'Wog,' Mum said. I stared at her disapprovingly. She explained: 'We tried every name we could think of and the only one he responded to was 'Dog', but we couldn't call him that, so we decided on 'Wog'; we thought it suited him.'

'Yeah,' I agreed, thinking that it was one of the ugliest names I had ever heard and it did suit this ugly skinny scratcher that was to become the ruination of my stockings. I wasn't wearing any at that moment but I was starting to teach in Ulverstone High in a few weeks. How could I avoid having to pay for new stockings all the time? I started plotting to get rid of him – maybe at the local dog pound.

Reading my thoughts Mum said: 'We couldn't turn him away.' She was always picking up waifs and strays, even people from the ships that called into Devonport.

I grimaced. Wog was obviously going to stay. I scowled at him threatening him with trouble if he didn't keep out of my way. He jumped up onto me again. I pushed him away roughly and stormed into the house.

The lazy weeks of my final holiday after uni ambled by, with Wog constantly interrupting my peaceful sunbathing or times spent sitting on the veranda reading to seek attention. I wasn't that upset when I dressed up, ready for my first school day. I was relieved I managed to run to the car before Wog could tear my stockings. When I came home, there he was again. He couldn't wait to scrape my legs and ruin the clothes.

I yelled at him. 'Get down!' but he took absolutely no notice.

'Get down!' I yelled more loudly, but still there was no reaction.

I lowered my voice. Perhaps he had had a man as his previous owner. 'Get down,' I growled, and he hesitated slightly. He didn't jump as high this time.

Eventually I perfected just the right tone and Wog stopped jumping at me. I had to keep shouting in a low demanding voice, 'Get down!' and my stockings were saved. Wog's antics after school reminded me of the lively teenagers in the classroom. I could hardly get a word in edgeways and my teaching was the worst ever. I tried this tone of voice and sure enough, after a tantrum or two, at least they gave me their attention, I demanded 'Sit down!' in the same tone of voice, and to my surprise they did.

I should have been grateful to Wog for teaching me this trick, but I wasn't. I never wanted the dog in the first place and by jumping at us all the time it wasn't the lovable intelligent dog Candles had been.

One holiday, as I was going away for a break in Nouméa, I snarled at Wog again and Dad smiled.

'We've found out why he jumps up all the time,' he said.

'Oh, why?' I asked just for politeness' sake.

'Yes, watch,' Dad said and held up a bit of sandwich he was eating. Wog jumped up and stood on his hind legs for some time while Dad moved the sandwich round and round. 'He dances for his supper!'

Sure enough, Wog wiggled from side to side in a kind of dance. I tried to show some enthusiasm, feeling slightly guilty about maligning the poor dog, but as he danced towards me I scuttled inside still plotting his disappearance. However, he stayed with us until the end of his life. I can't even remember what he died of – sorry Wog, you arrived at the wrong time in the wrong place. At least Mum and Dad loved you.

For our final years at university in Melbourne, my friends Anne, Jan and I decided to leave our college rooms and share a flat. We got one in the posh area of Parkville near the university. With my first glance at our sitting room, my shoulders drooped. It looked shabby and depressing. I was determined to improve it, so I bought some material and covered the armchair. It made things a little better.

Anne and I shared a room and we all took it in turns to cook and do the washing-up.

One evening, my arms were deep in soapy washing-up water and I looked at the huge pile of saucepans waiting to be washed. I never used THIS many saucepans when I cooked, I muttered to myself.

'Hey,' I yelled out to the other two who were lounging in the sitting room. 'I've got a brilliant idea.'

'Yeah?' Jan asked.

'Whenever it's our turn to get the dinner, let's make it our turn to do the washing-up as well'

'Oh? Why?' Anne asked.

'Because,' I said edgily, 'then there won't be so many saucepans to wash up!' I rattled another saucepan as I slung it crossly into the sink.

No one replied, but the rule was accepted from then on.

Chapter fifty-two

Things didn't always run smoothly.

As all university students do, we partied quite often. My bed was next to the door and was used as the place for everyone to put their coats.

At one particular party, the flat was full of voices and people were having a great time when suddenly I felt very ill and quite faint.

I staggered to the bedroom and stared at the pile of coats on my bed. I didn't have the strength to lift them, so I crawled under the covers and under the coats. I lay inert in the bed and no one noticed I was missing.

A loud jangling noise disturbed my sleep. It was the phone next to my bed. I could only just lift my hand. I struggled to take the receiver off the phone. I dropped it next to me so that I could speak into it and just hear who was calling.

'Hello,' I said weakly.

'Hi, It's Anne here.' It was my cousin Anne Hammond who was doing physiotherapy at the hospital in Melbourne.

'Hi,' I croaked.

'How are you? Everything's great here ...' she babbled. I listened and didn't even have the strength to tell her that I was very ill and wanted to cut the phone call short.

I just managed to lift the receiver back onto its cradle before I sank into a deep all-night sleep. I had no idea when people came to get their coats and if they saw me sleeping they certainly didn't wake me.

I'd hoped I would be better the next day – and I was. I never thought I should get to a doctor and nobody in the party seemed to notice that I was ill. They were all having such a good time – we never worried about seeing a doctor when we were students. We were young and would live forever.

It was when I was a student helping at a monastery on the Atherton Tableland in Queensland, Australia, that I had one of my many accidents. I was not hurt, but I made a terrible mistake.

We were having a lovely working holiday with the monks. They had an out-of-tune piano in the hall and during our breaks I enjoyed trying to pick out the latest pop tunes on the piano and find just the right harmony to get as close as possible to the real thing.

One of the jobs the monks gave us was painting the hall. The hall was rather large with very high walls and a lovely shiny wooden floor. I was to start painting from the top. Carrying an open pot of white paint and a paint brush, I shinnied up a very tall ladder to start work near the ceiling.

Unfortunately, I must have bumped it against one of the rungs of the ladder, for in a flash the open tin fell to the ground spreading a pool of white paint all over the shiny wooden floor. I was not popular. It took us a long time to clear up, and my relaxation times playing the very out-of-tune piano were cut short.

I've always had my clumsy moments. At primary school when I came second in a running race, Dad told me that he had been a very good athlete. While I had been good at running and most other sports, I could never be called 'graceful'.

When I lived in Peterborough in England, I joined the local theatre group and auditioned for a part in a play called *Charlie's Aunt*. They needed someone to play a graceful young lady. When I walked on the stage and said my lines, a voice from the darkness inside the theatre called out to me:

'Can you walk more gracefully that that?'

'No,' I said and finished the audition as best as I could.

They must have been desperate for someone to fill the part for I was still given it. I spent a few nights trying to be a little more graceful and to deliver my lines at the right time. This was not always easy for the chap playing 'Charlie's Aunt' threw himself into the comic part and made the audience laugh with his extra lines and added antics.

The kind examiner who came to Tasmania and gave me a great mark for my piano exam was Ronald Farren Price and after I had been accepted at Melbourne University to study music, with the piano as my major subject, he became my teacher. Wow! I was in love with this lovely person. He was so tall and so slim, and his graceful face and gentle voice made all our girls' hearts flutter. He had us all under his spell.

I had a piano lesson with him once a week except when he was touring the world giving piano concerts. The rooms were small and you had to open two doors before you could enter, for one of them was for soundproofed.

After one of my piano lessons, when he and I knew I needed to practise more, I was thrilled when he asked if I wouldn't mind bringing him up a cup of tea. I dashed downstairs, and with shaking hands carried the tea up to the room, swung open the door, stepped forward to give Mr Farren Price the cup of tea, and whallop! I had forgotten the sound proofing door. It swung hard into my elbow, and the cup shot forward and spilled tea all down Mr Farren Price's suit! I was SO embarrassed. He made me feel worse because he was so charming about it.

When I was in school, hockey was my favourite winter sport. I loved the feeling of the stick picking up the ball and flicking it forward for yards in one swift movement.

I practised and practised, turning up to all our practices on the field a short bus ride from school and from Madame George's home where I was staying. Come rain or shine, I was there, puffing around the field as we warmed up.

Never being a slim kind of girl, I always staggered onto the bus looking bright pink, but I didn't care. It was so exhilarating being able to keep up with the ball and pass it to the wing, and then being able to watch a girl scoop up the ball and dribble it all the way to the goal post and flick it in.

My job as centre half was to tackle the other team's centre and I was almost there. One day, when she got away from me yet again, stopped and hit the ball way down the field to her end, I had a brain wave. I realised that there was always a moment when your opponent didn't have her stick on the ball. When she raised her stick as high as she could before she hit the ball, the ball was all alone, perfectly free. I stood near her, waited for her to start raising her stick and with one quick push I pushed the ball away and towards one of my own team. It worked!

However, one day, I did the same trick but forgot something very important. The other player had stopped the ball and was about to hit it. I was very close and pushed the ball away quickly but forgot to move my leg. She brought the stick down as hard as she could, expecting to hit the ball. Instead, she hit me in the centre of my left leg, very, very hard. I was stunned, and my leg froze unable to move. The pain was excruciating. I couldn't join in the game for some time even though I pretended everything was fine. It was my fault after all.

Many years later, when I run my finger down the bone on my left leg I can still feel the hollow that the hockey player had made. Sometimes I can be too clever for my own good.

I had many other accidents but there are some events when sometimes things go wrong that are not your own fault, things that you have to suffer and learn how to deal with.

Chapter fifty-three

Mum's illness

As Mum entered her forties, she used to insist on a little nap after lunch and no one in her office seemed to mind. It wasn't until years later we realised she was seriously ill with cancer.

She always smoked. There was one famous occasion when she was much younger and standing next to Rae Birch, the mother of my best friend Jennifer Birch. When someone came along that Mum didn't want to know that she smoked, she made Rae hold her cigarette. Fortunately, Rae thought it was funny. I guess Mum was always up to mischief like that, so life was never dull when she was around.

As the years passed, Mum started coughing, not just once, but time and time again, and it often stopping her from speaking properly. I used to feel annoyed about it and say 'Go to the doctor'. She probably did go but there was nothing to be done. She asked me once, girl to girl, what she could do about the pain she felt – I was helpless and could only suggest asking the doctor. She found codeine helped a bit. When they finally operated on her they found it was far too late, as she was full of cancer that had originated as ovarian cancer. I only found this out much later. While I was at university Mum's played her illness down and I didn't think much about it. I knew, more than anything, Mum wanted, me to pass my degree for she'd never had the opportunity.

When I was 21, I had a party in our flat in Parkville Melbourne. Mum and Dad had come over to Melbourne but on the night of the party Mum couldn't come because she had a very heavy cold. I thought it was just a bit of a nuisance. After Mum and Dad returned to Tasmania, I continued my studies and practised hard for my final practical exams.

The day of my piano finals was looming fast. It was the next day and my friend Anne also had her final piano exam that day too. She and I were far too nervous.

'I can't stand it, I'm so nervous,' I said to Anne.

'I know what you mean,' she said.

'Let's go out and do something.' I couldn't wait to get outside in the fresh air. 'Let's go for a walk down Parkville Road.' The next thing I knew, we were arm in arm dancing Zorba the Greek's dance down the main road. Fortunately, there was not much traffic.

The next day arrived and it was my turn for my final piano exam. Heart thumping loudly and fingers trembling, I went into Melba Hall, the huge hall at Melbourne Conservatorium where all the important concerts were held. Three learned professors sat at the table, arms folded. I had to walk up onto the platform on my own in this huge concert hall and play all the pieces I had learnt.

One new technique that Mr Farren Price had taught me was how to relax when playing the piano. I was always very up tight and didn't know what he was talking about. He would make me rest my arm on his finger, and when he let his finger go, my arm was supposed to relalxed enough to drop to my side suddenly. When we first did it, he could take his finger away and my arm would stay there, in mid-air, for no way was I relaxed. However, we persisted and despite my practising for nearly five hours a day, getting my fingers so strong and quick they were fat with muscle, my arms were eventually relaxed and I no longer had this ache between my shoulder blades.

Could I relax while I was playing in my final exam? That was the challenge. While I was playing my pieces, I concentrated on this one thing. It stopped me panicking about all the other things that could have gone wrong. Nothing was said as I stumbled outside the hall. When I finally saw my results pinned up on the notice board, I had passed! Later I was told that the adjudicators had said how relaxed I was!

We had to study one subject that surprised me, Music and Movement. I was training to be a teacher, not a dancer but I had to prance around in a leotard marking time or inventing movements to the music. It was SO embarrassing.

The examination for this subject was even worse. There was one boy in our group who looked so gangly that I always thought he found this subject more difficult that the rest of us. He was not handsome like some students I quite fancied so I was horrified when we were partnered to do a dual act for our exam. I gritted my teeth, threw myself around, pretended I liked the chap and tried to fit in with his movements so that we looked as if we were working together. To my surprise, when I looked at my exam results for this subject, I could not find my name in any of the people who had passed. Surely I had not failed! This would mean I would have to do the exam again. I groaned. I glanced up at the people who got honours for the subject and to my surprise there was my name: Rosemary Hammond First Class Honours – WOW!

The other nerve-racking exam I did at this time was sight-reading. I think everyone hates sight-reading. You are given a piece of music you've never seen and you have to play it almost straight away.

I sat outside the examination room and watched one after another of us being called in for their turn. We were getting more and more nervous and so, when it was my turn and I heard 'Rosemary Westwell?', I marched in.

One of the examiners said in the kindest voice they could manage, 'Would you like to play the piece on the piano?'

I cheekily retorted, 'Not really, but I will if I have to!'

I then played very slowly and carefully making sure every note was correct. When I had finished, the examiner asked, 'And what do you think of the speed of the piece?'

'Oh, I played it FAR too slowly!'

I was very lucky the examiners let me pass that exam in spite of my cheekiness.

I still had a couple of written exams to do, and then my degree course would be finished and I could go home for a long holiday. I couldn't wait.

Then the phone rang.

It was Dad, 'Roe, your mum's gone. I was talking to the doctor and she just died.'

I froze, the receiver clutched in my hand. Mum, whom I knew was ill, but I hadn't really believed she was THAT ill, certainly not ill enough to die. She was far too young.

I spluttered, 'Yes – er, I'm sorry Dad,'

'Can you tell Aunty Joyce?' his voice was soft.

'Yes, of course,' I spluttered, 'and I'll come home now!' and put the phone down.

I waited for the news to sink in. It couldn't be true!

I had to tell Mum's sister, Aunty Joyce. Aunty Joyce, who had told me often how she had practically brought up Mum. She obviously loved her and was proud of the way Mum was such a good mother to us. I knew that Aunty Joyce would be terribly upset and I didn't know if I could deal with her reaction.

I chickened out and with my fingers shaking, I rang cousin Michael and his wife Hope. They were much more practical people and they looked after Aunty Joyce. I was so relieved when they said they would tell Aunty Joyce the terrible news.

I needed to be home, with Dad, now. I grabbed the phone book and started calling. The only plane I could get back from Melbourne to Tassie was a cargo plane which had seats for a few passengers.

'I'll take it!' I said. I would have taken anything if it would get me home soon.

Chapter fifty-four

One door closes and another opens

As if in a dream, I climbed on board the plane and sat at the window seat, did up my buckle and cried. I cried and cried. I decided to let the tears flow then rather than bottle everything up so that it would come out later.

I hardly noticed the figure seated next to me who was shifting nervously in his seat.

Eventually, it was too much for him

'Excuse me,' he said, 'Do you mind if I ask why you are crying so much?'

'My mum died,' was my curt reply.

He sat in silence for the whole of the trip while my tears continued to flow.

The house in Devonport felt cold and empty. Dad and I hugged for ages but said nothing. I slept in my bed in the attic in the room that Mum and Dad had decorated specially for me with green leaves stretching skywards on the wallpaper and a little pocket in the corner still not quite finished. I woke to find my pillow still wet with tears. Mrs Saul from over the road had come over to get our house straight for the visitors that would come later. She knew I wouldn't get around to doing anything like that.

The funeral was a blur. All I remember was not having any black clothes to wear so I wore my pink dress.

I remember distinctly the bright autumn sunshine as they lowered Mum's shiny coffin into the ground. I knew that would be the last time I would see her. I let out a painful sob and for the next few years this deep feeling of hurt infiltrated everything.

I just had one written exam to go for my degree, so I asked to have that postponed. I was tempted to give up my studies and go home to stay with Dad so that we could nurse our grief together, but I knew that Mum would have wanted me to finish my degree, so I went back to Melbourne to sit my final exam. The degree was finally mine.

At Melbourne University I was on a Commonwealth Scholarship which meant my tuition fees and living allowance were paid by the education department on condition that after four years of study I would return to Tasmania and teach for four years.

In those days the education department put you in a job – you had no real say where you went. I was given a job at Ulverstone High, not that far from home in Devonport, so I stayed with Dad in our large empty house and went to my first job.

It was awful to start with.

There was no special music room; any music we made would be heard by all the classes around. The walls and windows were thin. Every classroom had a little stage for the teacher to stand on and we had a blackboard and chalk to write up what we wanted the students to see or copy.

The classes were full of teenagers who wouldn't let you get a word in edgeways and they certainly didn't want to learn anything.

I tried everything. We had been told at university that music was just organised sound, and you could make up a piece using anything. I decided to do this in the classroom. Of course, these rowdy youths wanted a lot of noise and the piece we 'composed' consisted mostly of banging desks and shouting. They were mid-'composition' when the door to the classroom was flung open. An elderly teacher bellowed at the students telling them off for disturbing my lesson and saying that if they did it again, they would have him to deal with. I meekly tried to tell him they were making up a composition, but he didn't hear me. He was so angry that I didn't persist. The students were annoyed. It was obviously all my fault.

Then, I remembered my solution to a lack of control in the classroom: – I changing my tone of voice, as our little wild dog, Wog, had taught me.

But we had also studied Educational Psychology at university and although the lecturer was the most boring man I had ever come across, and sometimes I couldn't stand his dreary voice and walked out of his lectures, he did give some advice that I remembered. He had said it was best to give the students a say, using a democratic approach. He walked in front of the students in the front row, leant forward and said, 'Did you say something?'

The student blushed and said 'No'.

He used this as an example of how to intimidate the students, which you should not do, he said.

Looking at the noisy crowd of teenagers milling around the classroom ignoring me completely, I decided to use his technique, but not in the way he had described.

I stood on the teacher's stage, picked up a huge pile of books I should have been using in the lesson, slammed them down on the floor and screamed, 'I WILL not have this!'

There was a slight pause in the students' conversations. They were amazed that the mouse had roared. Apparently, I had stopped the whole school for a moment.

Anxious to grab the opportunity while I had it, I then used the tone Wog had taught me and said, 'Now SIT DOWN!'

From these shaky beginnings, my teaching career started.

Every morning I would get up early and dress for school in my freezing attic room. Dad was very proud of his off-peak heating, so I didn't like to say that it didn't work and I was shivering with the cold. There was no central heating in many houses in those days and although Dad had tried to plumb some in, apparently it was upside down and didn't work.

I would then crunch my way across a thick layer of frost that covered our back yard, climbed into Mum's Mazda car that I had inherited and drive along the beautiful sea coast to Ulverstone.

Every evening I came back exhausted and went through the motions of getting Dad and I our dinner – Mum-style: meat and three veg followed by a pudding. Dad decided that I really shouldn't have to do this and advertised for a cook to come and cook our evening dinner. I thought this was a bit unnecessary, but it was Dad's house, Dad's decision.

She arrived: a plumpish, pale almost elderly lady, pinny on and ready. I knew I was not a fantastic cook, but her meals were even worse than mine! When an over-grilled lamb chop arrived with a blob of Vegemite (Marmite in England) on top of it for the sauce, I complained. Dad, unabashed, said nothing and we sat at the dining table, Dad ringing his bell to summon our 'cook' when we wanted the plate taken away and our pudding served. I admired Dad's style but thought that maybe it was all a bit old-fashioned for the style of life people now led.

Chapter fifty-five

The moon and a star performance

In 1969 a teacher who lived close to the school in Ulverstone asked some of us if we would like to come and see a man landing on the moon for the first time. On her black and white TV, we saw this plump white figure float down the steps and make his little speech, 'One small step for a man one giant leap for mankind.'

I thought it sounded contrived and he must have practised what to say. He couldn't jump up and down and cry 'Wheee' which is what I would have done and was half expecting him to do.

There were a few interesting moments while I was at Ulverstone. I was told one of the students was great at singing pop, so I arranged for him to sing at Assembly. I didn't realise he would choose a song that was not particularly religious. It was in fact, 'The House of the Rising Sun' which was said to be about a prostitute's house! Our headmaster was rather a serious man and I had to stop myself from smiling as he sat on the stage watching a young lad traipse all over the stage with wires for his guitar and then hearing his specially produced gravelly pop voice ring out the story of a prostitute's house. He put on a good show, nevertheless.

When I had been at High School there were no music classes at all. The only music I had was my piano lessons. I had learnt the piano, singing and clarinet at university so I decided to start teaching some of the students these instruments. A kind volunteer who played the violin came and gave lessons in the lunch hour. Thus we formed a very small, quite unusual little orchestra; it was the best I could do.

After a year at Ulverstone High School I saw an information sheet that said if you had finished a Music degree at Hobart University, you would get a very large salary as a Music teacher.

I thought, 'Wait a minute, that salary is nearly double mine and I've been to an even better university than Hobart!'

I went to the headmaster to ask for an explanation. He said he would get back to me, and, sure enough they had not been paying me enough.

Suddenly I was in the money. Did I save it, or pay Dad back for keeping me so long? Not me. I decided to go on a trip to Noumea, in New Caledonia where they spoke French, so that I could try out the French I had learnt for A level.

I sat on the plane next to two very handsome Frenchmen and managed a little conversation. The best I could do was understand that they probably worked for a tyre company. No matter, I was on my way to having a lovely holiday.

The hotel was right by the sea. When I came down to breakfast I would watch the waves gently falling on the sandy shore not far from the open doorway and help myself to a green banana for part of my breakfast. I had to be persuaded that green bananas really were ripe.

I'd booked a trip to go inland and I joined a taxi with two other travellers. I had forgotten how car sick I used to get as a child and this crazy driver swooped around the tight corners on the road that meandered up the hillside. He drove so fast that I felt sicker and sicker. I shouted, 'Stop! I'm going to be sick!'

We stopped and I gingerly stepped out of the car, drew in a few breaths of air and only just managed to stop myself from being ill.

The rest of the holiday I visited places that reminded me of the tropical nature of Queensland. We saw a cagoo that was native to the islands and, like the kiwi of New Zealand, couldn't fly. I managed to practise some French but the couple I joined were from New Zealand spoke English so I ended up speaking English most of the time.

On the flight back I sat next to someone who worked for the government in New Guinea. I joked that I'd heard that there were still cannibals in New Guinea, so I hoped he would survive his next trip there. He turned the joke on me by saying that they had lost someone in the jungle some time back. To this day I don't know whether he was joking or not.

Our school terms were long and very tough, for we didn't have half-term breaks. One winter I counted fourteen weeks straight before we had any kind of a holiday. However, when we had a school holiday it lasted many weeks so I tried to go away.

One school holiday I booked to go on a bus tour of the vineyards in South Australia. On the bus was a dear old gentleman who turned out to be the grandfather of a student I taught. Although I didn't tell the grandfather, I remembered the student well for he was always complaining; even his fellow classmates were sick of him complaining and having to be the best. One day they had been in the examination hall doing their school exams when a bird managed to get in and it decorated the boy's exam paper. I'm sorry to say that we stifled our laughter as we went to help him.

His grandfather on the other hand was great fun and we both enjoyed learning about the history of the vineyards. I had never known before but many of the vineyards had been established by German families who knew the business well. However, I was NOT impressed when we were offered a sample of red liquid and find it was cordial! (Cordial is called squash in England.)

I had been told that I would only have to stay at Ulverstone High for one year, my probation year when I made all my mistakes (and, boy, did I make mistakes).

So I asked the man from the education department if I could go on to Devonport High because I'd heard that they needed a music teacher there.

He said 'No' and told me they had someone else in mind for that position.

I was furious. They had broken their promise! I then asked if they would pay the violin teacher and again they said 'No!'

That was enough! I'd had it. I was leaving even if I had to pay off my bond which was over £100.

Meanwhile I was having trouble with boyfriends. I was young and really wanted a decent boyfriend, but they were very hard to find.

Chapter fifty-six

Meeting a stranger in the night

One night I thought I had met the right person. Dad and I often went visiting and he had suddenly decided he wanted to go out to Hawley Beach to see a friend. I didn't really want to go but begrudgingly accompanied him. Some miles along the road, I got fed up and said I wanted to go back and if we didn't I would get out of the car. Dad knew how to deal with a spoilt girl and simply pulled up the car and let me out. There I was alone on the road in the dark, my white jumper reflecting in the moonlight as I watched Dad's car disappear over the horizon.

I shrugged my shoulders, turned and headed towards home, a trek of 12 miles or so. I could hear a car behind me. It gradually slowed down and stopped. The side door opened. It was a strange man offering me a lift. I knew you shouldn't climb into cars of strange men but, he looked alright and I really didn't want to walk 12 miles in the dark on my own, so I risked it.

He chuckled, 'What's a girl like you doing out alone on a night like this?'

'I've just had an argument with my dad,' I sulked.

He chuckled even more and eventually I felt brave enough to have a conversation with him.

He lived only a few doors away from our house! How amazing!

One day as I was fiddling about in the garden, he pulled up and invited me out to dinner.

Wow! This was better. I looked at him. Perhaps this was fate. He had a pilot's licence and could fly planes around Tasmania.

'Once', he said, 'I took a load of mutton birds to the mainland.'

'How interesting.'

'Interesting maybe,' he said, 'but they stank horribly! I could hardly breathe.'

I investigated these mutton birds. There was no internet in those days. I only had Arthur Mee's Encyclopaedias or the butcher. Eventually I bought a mutton bird to cook– a plump brown bird with a long thin beak.

It was a bit greasy, so I put it in the oven and baked it, waiting until the fat had fallen from the bird so that we could eat the meat. I waited and waited. The bird had been in the oven for four hours and it was STILL too fatty. I gave up, threw it out and we never tasted it.

I thought our romance was well and truly made when he invited me on one of his flights, without the mutton birds, I was assured. I was so excited.

The day of my first flight with my new boyfriend arrived. The sun was shining, the sky was blue and my heart was beating fast as I saw his car pull up outside my house. He drove me to the aerodrome over the bridge to East Devonport on the other side of the river. We arrived, he went into the office and talked while I hung about outside. It was a very small aerodrome and I knew it well from the times I had flown to and from university in Melbourne.

He took me to a little Cessna, a tiny plane that sat down on the grass. He tested the fuel and various other things until he said it was time to go and I could get in. I clumsily clambered into the seat. He got into the pilot's seat and everything was wonderful. The plane lifted up easily and soon we were flying high in the sky. I could feel the wind in my hair as I looked down. Devonport and the coastline looked like they were in a picture. The white houses with red corrugated rooves looked like dolls' houses, and the big green paddocks made a lovely quilt of different greens and browns. The cliffs and the sea below sparkled in the sun.

He flew us along the coast, past the towns of Burnie and Penguin. He said he needed to touch down near Wynyard. I didn't think anything of it. I thought it was something to do with the plane. Then I looked down and saw two girls standing in the paddock looking up at us. I was puzzled.

He landed the plane perfectly. Then came a shock I had NOT been expecting. In a matter-of-fact voice he said, 'This where you get out and wait while I give these girls a flight too.'

Open-mouthed, I clumsily clambered out of my seat and stared as the two girls climbed into the plane. Arms folded, I glared as the plane lifted up into the sky.

It was then that I knew this new 'boyfriend' was not for me.

The trouble with Devonport and Tasmania is that they are far too small. Wherever I went, I would bump into people, including this non-boyfriend. The only sensible thing to do was for me to leave and seek my fortune in another country.

Chapter fifty-seven

Con

While I waited to get all the paperwork ready I met a lovely Greek boy called Constantinos and we started going out. His parents had decided on his future wife back in Greece, so we knew nothing would come of our relationship. He was amazing. He was short, but very strong and wiry with curly black hair and dark brown eyes. He could speak English very well (as well as Greek, of course) and he was even studying ancient Greek. He did this while he worked for the Hydro Electric Commission which built huge dams in the centre of Tasmania and used water power to provide electricity.

His living quarters were not a house or a hostel. All he had was a little wooden shed. He said he was trying to earn money to send home.

He was always involving himself in hobbies. One day he took me away to the south of Tasmania where we searched for fossilised manfern. A manfern tree looks like bracken that has grown into a huge tree. Millions of years ago, the trees fell and turned to stone. Tasmania is one of only about three places in the whole world where you can find fossilised manfern. I have a piece that a kind friend who collects gems gave to me. You can see the rings of the inside of the fern in the hard, polished stone.

The other stones my Greek friend collected were agates which were not so valuable, but very beautiful. He made me a necklace with a piece of agate on it.

By now Dad had bought a white Jaguar sports car. I am told it was a K140. It was long and low, had beautifully rounded features and was lovely to drive.

Dad was a little unwilling to let me drive it.

'It's too heavy for you, isn't it?' he asked.

'No, not at all!' I replied.

'Well, you have to double declutch.'

'What's that?'

Dad showed me, and I was determined to get the hang of it. Soon I could put my foot down and up and down again on the clutch to engage the gears. No problem.

I loved my hair being ruffled and the feel of the fresh air sweeping my face as I zoomed over the green hills of Tasmania.

My Greek friend Con spent months doing up his own white Sprite sports car and soon there were two white sports cars outside our place. Yes, I thought, this is the way to live!

One evening Con and I went to a party and it lasted so long that we had stayed up all night. As we drove in his sports car along the beautiful coast, I sat back in my seat and gazed at the thin stretch of light as dawn approached. I decided that this had been one of my best evenings ever. My eyes closed a little. I was looking forward to sleep.

'We've been invited to breakfast on Hawley Beach,' Con shouted above the roar of the engine.

Sleep would have to wait. 'Great!'

We pulled up outside a small shack and were met by Rex Harrison, well someone who was SO like him. Rex Harrison was a very famous actor who played a professor teaching a Cockney girl from London how to speak and dress properly in a film called *My Fair Lady*. In those days, everyone knew *My Fair Lady*.

I was told that this man had indeed been Rex Harrison's stand-in – well that was the story. After a lovely breakfast of eggs and bacon, I climbed into Con's sports car and he drove me home. I slipped through the front door at about seven in the morning, crept upstairs, changed into my nightdress and had a little bit of a sleep. Later, I came down for breakfast as usual and waited for Dad to ask where I'd been.

He didn't. He hadn't even noticed that I'd been out!

Chapter fifty-eight

Uncle Chappy and more change

Mum's brother was called Uncle Chappy. He was a very short, rotund gentleman who took an interest in me, his young niece, as I grew up.

Once he took me with him around Tasmania to check up on people who were supposed to have had an X-ray to look for tuberculosis.

On one visit we called at a dilapidated farm. The buildings were made of plain wood and some of the panels were slipping. A scrawny weather-beaten man came to the door and spoke to Uncle Chappy. I'msure he said: 'I don't need no checks, I'm OK. I use sheep dip.'

Uncle Chappy decided to take Dad and me out for a posh drink at the Formby Hotel down by the river in Devonport. He introduced us to a special drink he had invented. He called it 'Ocean Romance' and it had nearly everything alcoholic in it: brandy, crème de menthe and advocaat at least. It was green and very tasty although it was wise to have only the one drink.

I'd decided if I had to leave Tasmania, I could have gone to the mainland, but I thought I may as well go all the way across the world to England.

My granddad who had come from England talked about Yorkshire sometimes and Dad always warned us not to say anything against Granddad's home in England.

Other relatives often spoke about the 'old country' (England) and most of the books we had at school talked about beech trees and things that I had never seen in Tasmania because they belonged to the old country. In the back of my mind was a curiosity that had started when I first saw a drawing of a beech tree in one of our reading books at primary school. This curiosity grew and grew until I really wanted to see the old country for myself.

In those days a girl didn't normally travel alone, but I wasn't going to let a little custom like that stop me.

While still driving to work in Ulverstone, I planned my escape. I had several injections against diseases that were abroad but not in Tasmania, including one to prevent yellow fever and another typhus. I had to have a certificate with my passport to say that I'd had the injections. The day after having two injections, one in each arm, my arms hurt and I had to conduct our little orchestra. It was very painful every time I tried to lift my arms!

The big day eventually came, and I was ready for adventure. Dad drove me to the airport in East Devonport. I hugged him and climbed on board.. I flew to Melbourne to catch the ship that was going to take me all the way to England.

The ship was a rusty old Greek one called the Australis. When I was on board, many of the other passengers held on to one end of streamers and their friends and family held the other. They kept hold of them until they broke as the ship was easing out of the port.

I took an anti-sickness pill, tried to ignore the horrible smell of the black smoke coming out of the funnel and went down to my cramped cabin.

When I got over my sea sickness and felt more normal, I went back on deck and took a seat at the bar. The waiter came and asked me what I would like to drink. I thought of the fantastic drink Uncle Chappy had introduced me to.

'I'll have an Ocean Romance,' I said. The waiter stood still for a moment, the tray shaking a little, before he said, 'Pardon?'

'An – then I realised, he thought I meant the real thing, an ocean romance. No wonder he didn't know what I was talking about. I corrected myself,

'A brandy and dry, please.'

At meal times, I found myself sitting with a group of strangers. We chatted and became friends. We had hours to kill while on board. I joined in the deck games trying to stop myself from breathing in too many of the smelly fumes from the funnels and, in the ballroom, practised Zorba's dance with one of the instructors. This brought back fond memories of dancing with my Greek friend Con who had shown me some of the steps. He had also explained to me that it was only the men who were supposed to dance, but here on board ship it didn't seem to matter.

Sometimes I would go up on deck and lean over the rail to see the water rushing past and breathe in the fresh sea air, trying not to be put off by the funnel smoke.

Chapter fifty-nine

Flying fish and flying fingers

One day, just above the water I could see fish flying. These fish really did 'fly' as I had been told. They popped up out of the water and sped a few inches above it and dived back in again.

While exploring the ship I found a piano in the ballroom. There was no one else there during the day and the only sound was the clattering in the kitchen the other side of the room. The lid was up and the piano keys beckoned. I can rarely resist a piano sitting all alone, unoccupied and unplayed.

I took a chance, sat down and played through all the pieces I had learnt. It was lovely to relax into my cosseted world of music, letting all my feelings flow through my fingers, feelings that I didn't have to share with anyone or try to explain.

My favourite pieces were the first movement of Beethoven's 'Moonlight Sonata', Chopin's 'Revolutionary Study', Rachmaninov's 'Prelude in C sharp minor' and Debussy's 'Clair de Lune'.

Even though the clattering in the kitchen increased and I heard some derogatory shouts from the kitchen, I ignored them; they would not spoil my moments of pleasure.

Worried that I might have caused some trouble, I asked my friends,

'What's up with the waiters? They don't seem a very friendly lot.'

'Oh, they're no worse than usual' replied John, a small bald-headed chap next to me. 'I saw one with his hand bandaged and when I asked why, I was told there had been a fight in the kitchen.'

'Mm.' I focused on my soup deciding I wouldn't make a point of befriending the waiters. 'If you want something to worry about,' said Chaz, a young wiry chap sitting opposite, 'apparently there was a fire on board this ship on its the last journey.'

'Really?' I paused. Determined not to be scared, I added, 'But it's still standing, so I reckon we'll be OK'.

Chapter sixty

The equator

One day passed like another on our four-week trip across the Pacific Ocean. As we came near the equator the sea was endless and we could see no land at all. It was easy to imagine how awful it had been for the sailors in the last century when ships only had sails and, when there was no wind, got stuck on the ocean for weeks.

There was a big announcement. We were about to cross the equator and there was a ceremony. You cannot see any sign of an equator on the sea. The only indication we had was the ship's daily newsletter. We had two newsletters for what seemed like the same date. We had crossed the date line.

King Neptune in a long flowing wig and trailing seaweed arrived at the edge of the ship's pool and plunged in – that was about all of the ceremony I remember.

I ganged up with three others as you have to get on if you are in one place for weeks with only one set of people.

The ship called into a few ports – Acapulco and Miami were the most memorable ones. We went through the Panama Canal and they kept telling us about a donkey that was pulling us as we slowly crept through the canal. I looked for an animal but it was a crane that was helping us get through the canals.

Before we stopped at Acapulco, we had been on board our ship for weeks. Every night for tea we were given an orange, so that we wouldn't get scurvy – something sailors used to get if they didn't have any vitamin C. (It's still possible to get scurvy these days if you don't eat any fresh food.) After weeks of eating these oranges, we began to hate their texture and decided that all we wanted was a juice squeezer so that we could enjoy, once and for all, some real juice.

When we arrived in the port of Acapulco, the first thing I noticed was the SMELL. In those days there were open sewers and in this hot place the smell was ghastly. It seemed so strange that this place, where all the famous film stars lived or visited, should smell so horrible. Didn't they notice?

We stood for a while admiring the sunlit harbour and the huge sailing boats, and for a few moments we thought we saw the famous film star John Wayne out on his boat. We didn't gaze out to sea for long, for in the short time we had in the port we wanted only one thing: a juice squeezer.

We tried in every shop, but we didn't speak Spanish and no matter how many different actions my friend John did, pretending to squeeze a lemon, we failed in our mission. There was no internet in those days, no Google to search to find out what we should have asked for was an 'exprimidor de limon'. We had to endure the oranges for the rest of the journey.

Miami was just like we had seen in the movies – huge houses (single storey houses I later learned to call 'bungalows' in England) with carefully tended lawns and palm trees reminding us it was a warm climate.

We hired a car and went on a trip to the Everglades National Park. I noticed that the police were very quick on their motorbikes and wore guns strapped to their belts. We were very lucky no policemen were watching us over the first few miles before we realised we were driving on the wrong side of the road – we were driving on the left but they drive on the right in America.

I wasn't sure I wanted to explore the Everglades too much for we were told it was full of alligators.

Chapter sixty-one

England!

As we came closer to Great Britain it got colder and colder. I was very eager to take my first step on England where my ancestors had come from and where there were many, many places I wanted to see.

One night I was out on deck and little flecks of cold ice were in the rain. 'What's that?' I asked. I'd never seen it before. 'It's sleet, snow that melts as it falls.' Wow! the first sign of snow, real snow.

I finally arrived in London. I had no real sense of money in those days and had plenty at first. I'd booked into the Royal Overseas League Hotel as a young lady should and stayed there until I settled in. It was very expensive and I wouldn't dream of staying there for any length of time now.

I bought a lovely warm brown full-length coat and thick black boots and I can remember now the excitement I felt as I trudged through London in real snow. It was like being in Dicken's novels. I was walking past all those famous places: Piccadilly Circus with Eros, Regent Street, Bond Street, Oxford Street – all the places I had learnt about when playing Monopoly in Tasmania.

I wanted to see Harrods. I realised that I needed to get a job soon if the money was going to last. Why not get a job at Harrods? I lined up with some forty other people after filling in and handing in our application forms.

Suddenly I was called to the front. They were very interested in my music degree and before I knew it, I was in a little room being trained to sell bikinis and tops in Harrods. I'd got a job but it was nothing to do with music.

Now I began to see what it was like to do a real job, to work long hours for little pay. I had to pay for my own uniform of a navy suit. I worked an eight-hour day and extra on Wednesday evenings and on Saturdays. I found a room to rent in Holland Park and I had to buy my own TV. I got up early, rushed for the bus and caught it to Kensington where I walked through the underground tunnel and into Harrods.

I hardly went out at all in the little spare time I was given, for I was living on minus 50p a week.

The only joy I really had was meeting typically English people such as an eccentric tailor who had worked at Harrods for years and who resented the new ways and the new foreign boss. I also saw a few famous people who came to the store. I served Telly Savalas, a famous film star who played an American detective who sucked a lollipop and said 'What's up baby?' He was with a slim red-haired lady. I couldn't see her left hand to see if she was married but he was too smooth by half.

'Whatever you want darling,' he said to her.

Another assistant sold Joyce Grenfell a new blouse for her to wear on TV the next day. Joyce was apparently very, very nice.

Then there was the chauffeur who came complete with uniform including jodhpurs calling for his mistress's package.

I had to keep a straight face when a lady wanted a tiny packet containing a pair of knickers delivered to her house. She could easily have popped them into her bag, but I guessed she wanted her neighbours to see the Harrods' van call.

I started chatting to a lady who seemed to be there quite often. She eventually told me she was the store detective so she couldn't speak to me too much. Then I told her about something very strange I had once seen but done nothing about for I was very new at the time. A tall man wearing a long black coat had been hovering around the swimsuits and I'd seen what looked like a bra strap coming out of his coat.

'Yes,' she said. 'Some of our swimsuits have gone missing.'

Another time, I was putting through a purchase on a credit card and the name on the card and the address she gave looked familiar. I glanced at the woman and she had a very straight innocent face. I decided the card must be alright. It was only later that I learned that someone had stolen the credit card we had been using to practise on when we were being trained.

I'd said I would stay at Harrods for at least three months and although I would have loved to have left earlier, I made sure I stayed those three months before giving in my notice. It was an eye-opener for me that some people had no choice but to take shop work. They had no other qualifications to fall back on whereas I took these different jobs for the experience, in the back of my mind knowing I could always go back to teaching if everything else failed.

Chapter sixty-two

Madame Tussaud's

I wanted to see Madame Tussaud's for free, so I applied for a job there. I got one in the kitchens serving ice cream and, as luck would have it, I had to stand next to the back door which was kept open even in the middle of winter! I wanted to work in the sweet shop where it was warmer and eventually got a job there.

I had a lot of sums to work out and it was a challenge. Australia had only just changed from pounds, shillings and pence to dollars and cents. Now Great Britain was changing from the pounds, shillings and pence that I knew, to pounds and new pence.

Then there was the language problem. Everyone spoke English, but they used a different English to me.

A little girl came up to the counter.

'I want a lolly,' she said. For me, a lolly was a sweet. 'Yes, what would you like?' I asked. 'Liquorice or bonbons, what would you like?' 'I want a lolly!'. I offered all the different kinds of sweets we had. She stamped her little foot, looked at me as if I was very peculiar and shouted. 'One of those, look!' she pointed to a picture on the wall. 'Oh,' I said, 'You want an icy pole. Why didn't you say?'

At the end of one day, I was one penny out on the till. My time was up and I had to find another job.

I went to work in an office for Camden Council and the job was so boring that I won't say any more about it. Even though I was working all the time, London was so expensive that my money was running out. I decided to go on one last journey around Europe, before I reluctantly tried to go back to teaching and earn a proper living.

Chapter sixty-three

Camping around Europe

It was the 1970s and I joined a firm named 'Adventure International' and, with ten others, climbed into a bus and set off around Europe. We had a leader to drive us to various camp sites and help us put up tents. We all took it in turns to do the cooking and the washing-up.

While I can't remember every detail, I do remember visiting Barcelona, Berlin, Budapest, Czechoslovakia, Florence, Grindelwald, Lauterbrunnen, Lucerne, Marseilles, Munich, Paris, Pisa, Rome, Salzburg, Sorrento (but not Etna), Venice and Vienna. It was very exciting to have something new to see and do every day. I was able to see all the places I'd heard about for so long when I was growing up in Tasmania.

However, this trip was, most of all, a learning experience. Not only was I learning more about the places and seeing for myself how they really looked and how the people lived, I was learning about myself. I had to get on with a group of people I'd never met before and who I didn't necessarily like but they would be my companions for a long time.

When I was growing up, people had often talked about how travel knocked the chips off one's shoulder and this trip, above all, did that for me. I grew up at last and instead of being grumpy and spoilt all the time, I mucked in, worked and enjoyed it.

If the majority of us wanted to go somewhere in the city where we had stopped, then we organised a trip. This worked well at first.

In Paris, we saw Montmartre where all the painters hung out and I was able to buy some prints to hang up on my wall in my flat. I even hired a room with a piano to practise on and imagined I was a poor composer like Debussy, having a rare treat for a day.

In Barcelona, I had the chance to see the weird architecture of Gaudi (I wasn't impressed – it looked like an overgrown ice cream cone) and I bought my guitar. It sounded lovely even though the back was made of two pieces of wood on and I knew that one piece would have been better. I still have that guitar now and one holiday when staying with friends in Essex many years later, I taught myself how to strum chords so I could accompany the singing when I was teaching while looking at the pupils.

In and near Marseilles, I couldn't believe it when a poor young lady in our group wasn't allowed to rest when she was feeling ill because they hadn't brought any cash to pay for the beach. I went into the famous casino of Monte Carlo and, using a method I had learnt in Tassie, managed to treble my money. It was a pity I was only using centimes, (pennies). I thought I would be in a room playing roulette with everyone dressed up and posh-looking, but I was a tourist and had to stay in the tourist area full of seedy looking down-and-outs and one-armed bandit machines. I watched while someone used a machine for a long time and won nothing. I then stepped forward, put one coin in and won a big prize, which I promptly spent.

We visited Rome where the girls among us had to wear something over our shoulders and our heads to go into the Cathedral. I was surprised that the Vatican City seemed so separate from the city of Rome. In Rome, I tried to buy a pair of sandals, but the shop seller had other ideas. In the end, a complete stranger and I battled to keep the man from giving us a kiss until we both gave up and ran out of the shop with nothing.

I remember one romantic evening on the hills of Sorrento watching a pale warm sunset and speaking to a lovely young man who was not so demanding.

We had planned to visit Etna but the volcano was live and threatening to erupt so we didn't go.

I marvelled at the lovely statues of Florence and the beautiful view across the city with all the orange rooves looking the same.

In Venice, we saw the gondoliers and intertwining canals with their quaint little bridges. We watched an expert glassmaker make all kinds of vases and glasses. We also visited St Mark's Square with all its pigeons and saw the magnificent Doge's Palace.

In Hungary, we visited the capital city Budapest and found out that Buda and Pest were two cities combined into one. Thinking there were very few people about, I was startled by a stranger who asked me to be his pen friend. I was a little wary for at this time Hungary was under communist control so I didn't agree to write to him.

Chapter sixty-four

Trying to keep out of trouble

I also knew I had to be careful when we visited Czechoslovakia especially after our rather embarrassing arrival. All the time we were travelling, I loved trying to use the little language I knew in the different countries. German seemed to be the most useful and because I knew a few words, I was asked to try to translate when we arrived at the Czech border. It was midnight and pouring with rain so we were anxious to get through. I was pushed to the front when the guard barked German at the leader. The leader didn't understand and unfortunately, I didn't either, so when the guard barked at me, I shrugged my shoulders indicating 'maybe'.

Suddenly the guard was angry and with shouts and wild hand signals he told us all to get off the bus immediately and the bus was searched from top to bottom. Everyone glared at me and eventually the leader worked out what had been asked.

We had been asked if we had any weapons and 'maybe' was NOT the right answer.

We stopped at a poorly equipped camp, where the cold showers had no curtains so we could easily be seen standing naked. In the restaurant I chatted as best I could in German to a young man and he spoke in hushed tones about how they had been forced to learn German at school and that we shouldn't really be talking for he would get into trouble. This was one of the first times I had an inkling of what it was like living in an undemocratic country where people could not vote for who ruled them.

It was even sterner in Berlin and in East Germany when we travelled there. In those days Berlin was divided into two, West Berlin was the democratic side and East Berlin along with East Germany was controlled by the communists. People had been known to disappear in East Germany, and some had been shot and killed as they tried to cross the border to West Berlin.

The Americans had set up a checkpoint on the border where westerners like us had to give our names. They could then check that we arrived back safely after visiting the communist side of Berlin.

At the border, the eleven of us started filing through. Suddenly the guard stopped me and barked 'Haben Sie Zeitungen?'.

Fortunately, this time I knew he had asked –if I had any newspapers with me. I was able to answer a firm 'No!' and reassure him that I had no propaganda for the East Berliners about how much better life was on the other side.

As we entered the eastern side of the city it was like entering a time warp. The few cars that were there were terribly old-fashioned and the people gathered in small groups on the pavements looked very grey, poor and depressed. Even worse, some houses had been split into two by a huge wall that was a barrier between the two sections of the city. I couldn't believe anyone could do this to a city and its people, and I was reminded why Dad had gone to war. If he hadn't, we could have all been living like this at home.

We were taken to places where only tourists were allowed to go and we had lunch in a restaurant. I gave more money than I needed to pay my bill and waited for the change. I should have realised it would never come, for the people were desperate for western money to buy western things.

Camping in West Berlin, I noticed that a helicopter flew over the border again and again. I wanted to see the opera in Berlin, but no one else did so the leader wasn't organising a trip. My obstinacy rose to the fore and I said, 'I'm going on my own then!' I managed to get the right bus to the opera house, thoroughly enjoy the concert and get back to the campsite in one piece. It was worth it.

When we travelled through East Germany, I was reminded again of the stark difference between the two different sides of the country. We stopped for a break at one of the 'cafés' and had to line up with a host of workers all in dungarees to get a meagre snack of hard black bread.

Vienna and Salzburg were much brighter, happier and livelier places. I could easily imagine the young Mozart enjoying life there. I liked his music although it was a bit strait-laced for me, and I preferred the later Romantic period. I did like Mozart's C minor piano concerto, however, which I'd tried to learn to play with the Harrods orchestra when I was there. As a soloist should, I'd learnt the music off by heart but the conductor hadn't liked the way I phrased it. I believed, and still believe, the orchestra should follow the interpretation of the soloist, and the strange way she wanted me to lift the phrases and cut them off too short irritated me. I decided not to continue.

In Vienna, I saw a real 'glockenspiel' made of a line of bells – for 'Glock' means 'bell' in German and 'spiel' means 'play', and the percussion instrument known as a 'glockenspiel' has a string of metal bars of different lengths representing the bells. I was also fascinated by the magnificent trained horses and the Viennese Waltz.

We went to a restaurant to hear the Viennese Waltz played and we sat at tables that had phones on them. The phone on our table rang. I thought 'how strange' and ignored it. Afterwards someone hissed at me – the man over there was trying to ring you, why did you ignore him?

We'd all heard of the Munich beer festival, so we sampled a litre jug of beer and sang together 'Ein Prosit, ein Prosit, der Gemütlichkeit' which means something like 'a toast to happiness' which I was all for.

In Switzerland, we saw the huge lake at Lucerne and camped between two huge mountains at Lauterbrunnen. The air was very fresh and cool. I glanced up the high cliff next to the campsite.

'Is that a goat up there?'

'Yes, there are a lot of mountain goats in Switzerland.'

I could hardly believe the goats as they scrambled up the very narrow paths on such very high, steep cliffs.

On a field nearby, we saw edelweiss and cows with bells reminding us of the famous film *The Sound of Music*.

Amsterdam meant we visited Anne Frank's house which was much less crowded than it is these days. Anne Frank wrote a diary when she and her family were hiding from the Germans. The family were eventually found by the Germans and sent to a concentration camp where Anne died.

During this trip, I had been trying out the ice cream in every country and I decided that Dutch ice cream was the best.

Chapter sixty-five

Trying to get back to work

Back in England I realised that I had no choice; I had to go back to teaching. I started applying for jobs. Fortunately, at that time, the headmasters could choose the teachers they wanted to work for them. After going on a number of interviews but not getting the jobs despite my qualifications, , I asked the headmaster in Cumbria, 'Why am I not getting the jobs I apply for?'

He said: 'It's easy. You're Australian and can't be trusted.'

I was amazed and a little offended, but then he had spoken plainly and I think he meant that we Australians are wanderers and cannot be trusted to stay for long.

So, I immediately applied a philosophy of life that has pulled me through even the most difficult of times: 'Turn a disadvantage to an advantage'.

I decided to apply for jobs in nice places so that I could go on interesting trips at the education department's expense, staying in lovely hotels, eating lovely meals, going for the interviews and failing to get the jobs and then finally going back to Australia.

I had a lovely weekend up in Windermere staying at the Applegarth Hotel and as planned, I didn't get the job. Then I got caught in Peterborough. The headmaster was obviously desperate for a music teacher and asked me if I had any other interviews that day. It was as if he could see through me. I had to admit I had one at Broadstairs later that afternoon. (I'd wanted to see where the Prime Minister Ted Heath lived.) He asked me for the phone number of the contact there, phoned and cancelled my appointment, and offered me the job in Peterborough. I didn't have enough money to pay for my expenses and turn the job down, so I had to accept. I was pleased to have a job at last, and not too disappointed that my plan to see the country had to stop.

Orton Longueville Comprehensive School had just been formed by combining a grammar school and a secondary modern school. English grammar schools taught the more academic and more privileged children, and secondary modern schools taught those who were more interested in practical subjects or who couldn't get into the grammar school. The children from the grammar school still wore their smart blue-striped jackets and I loved the idea of teaching in a real English school, having half-term holidays and living in a village called Orton Waterville which had lovely thatched cottages.

It even snowed while I was there, and the neighbours thought I was odd offering to dig out the snow from their drives. While it was not always easy teaching in the comprehensive school, it was certainly no worse than teaching in Tasmania.

However, the language problem became obvious again. I was teaching a class of teenagers. I showed them a picture of an orchestra and told them to stick the pictures in their books. I thought I'd told them to use plenty of sticky tape. They all roared with laughter and some of them could not stop giggling. I thought they hadn't heard me, so I repeated it and said they had to use it all along the top, down the sides and along the bottom of the picture to make sure it was stuck properly in their exercise books.

By now the class was beside itself but I had to wait until break to find out what had happened. When I told the staff what I'd said, they too roared with laughter. In Tasmania, the word we use for sticky tape is 'durex' which everyone in England knows as something to stop you having babies.

Chapter sixty-six

Peterborough

When I first came to Peterborough, I had nowhere to live so I put an advertisement in the local newspaper for a room. A delightful farming family called the Darbys replied and I was thrilled to find that the room was in the old manor at Paston Ridings near Peterborough. I was to live in the middle of real history. The room was huge, and they had gone to a lot of trouble to redecorate it. I stood at the window and looked out at the grass and trees; this was no tiny box room. I was sharing the house with the grandmother, Mrs Darby, and she was a real treasure.

'What can I do for you?' she kept asking, her voice gentle and her warm round face smiling.

'What would you like for tea?' she asked every night when I came back from school – even though I understood I was supposed to get my own food. I even caught her lugging in a huge scuttle of coal. 'Here, let me take it!' I said in alarm as this little eighty-year-old struggled. She would have none of it. At last I felt comfortable, relaxed and at home.

I wanted to meet more young people like myself. I quite liked the grandson of the family. He was handsome in a very English way and I was thrilled when he asked me to accompany him to a posh wedding. I was very nervous and felt a little out of depth with all these wealthy families. We spoke a little, but there was no spark, sadly.

Then I joined The Young Conservatives' Club, not because I was going to vote conservative, but because this was a club for young people. One evening I had arranged with a friend called Dave to play mini-golf. Dave and I were about to move from the bar when a short, smiling stranger with a moustache butted in. 'Hello, Dave,' he said, clapping Dave on the shoulder. 'How are you?'

'Fine. I hear you've been to Toronto.'

'I've just arrived back. It was tremendous, you've never seen so many tall buildings. What are you doing?'

'Oh, we're about to play mini-golf.'

'Come on, then,' said the stranger, and he and Dave moved off to play.

I stood there alone, fuming. I was determined this new upstart was not going to forget me, so when the group met at the pub later I accosted him and said, 'I'll have you know you interrupted my game of mini-golf with Dave!'

'Did I? I'm so sorry,' smiled the stranger, a smile that I will never forget. That was the beginning.

A few nights later he phoned the manor house and, much to my embarrassment, my landlady's grandson answered the phone and took a message.

Chapter sixty-seven

John

Your granddad John and I went on our first date.

'What would you like to drink?'

'A brandy and dry please.'

'A brandy and what?'

'A brandy and dry,' I repeated.

'What's a "dry"?'

'You mean you don't know?' I drawled in my Australian accent. 'A dry ginger ale, of course!'

This was the drink I'd been used to in the days when Dad kept me and I had no real idea of costs. Brandy is not the cheapest drink, so your Granddad John gulped and bought me not one, but by the time the evening had finished, three. He certainly didn't forget me and soon after he asked me away for the weekend.

By now I'd learnt that you always go prepared for disaster. With enough money for a taxi home, I climbed into his Ford Escort and we drove south to Essex.

Chapter sixty-eight

Essex

The sun lit up the fields of wheat as your Granddad John drove along the narrow winding roads in Essex. Field after field of gold stretched beside us and rows of little thatched cottages with pale pink walls smiled at us as we swept past. I felt part of the world of Constable's paintings. I almost expected us to come across a horse and cart with the trailer bulging with harvested wheat. However, we didn't meet any other cars or transport and soon pulled into the yard of a lovely English thatched cottage. After the crowded polluted months I'd spent in London, this was heaven, but it wasn't the place we were looking for.

I saw a signpost. 'Haven't we been here before?' I was sure I'd already seen the sign to Broxted two or three times.

'Er yes.'

'You mean you're lost?' I could hardly believe it!

'I'm afraid so. Don't worry, I think it's this way.'

We drove along some very narrow lanes to a gorgeous little village. We swept across a narrow little bridge and up a hill with trees hugging each side of the narrow road. I was holding my breath praying that we didn't meet any other cars on the way, for there was no room for them. John hooted the horn at each junction.

Eventually, we pulled into the yard of a very old house, with the plastered walls and a tiled roof. A lovely couple, John's best friends, met us with warm smiles and we were soon enjoying a cup of Earl Grey tea and Madeira cake.

John and I had only just met so we had separate rooms. The dark narrow staircase led to a wooden door that John opened with a clunk. The latch was like the ones we used to have on our lavatory doors in the house in Victoria Parade. I loved this medieval-style living. I dumped my bag and rushed to the window. It had small panes of glass and through it I could see some huge ancient trees on the other side of the road. The birds were singing their hearts out. This was bliss.

The next day we went harvesting. How wonderful to be a part of real country life, something that had been going on for centuries, well before any white man had set foot on Tasmanian shores.

Bales of hay lay scattered over the stripped fields of gold. Our job was to collect them, put them on the trailer and bring them back to the farm to stack in the barn. I was warned that I needed strong gloves and resilient clothes. Straw is not soft and gentle as I had imagined; it scratched. I stabbed the bales with the pitchfork, bent my knees and put my weight under each bale, hoisting it high and dumping it on the trailer for a farm hand to add it to the neat pile that was growing at the back.

I was asked if I had ever driven a tractor.

'No,' I said, 'but I drive a car'. I couldn't see the difference. 'I'd love to drive the tractor!'

So I sat on the rather flimsy seat, listened as I was told where the accelerator and the brake were and started the engine. It was a bit bumpy at first as I tried to judge how hard to push the accelerator. We moved slowly forward. Every now and then, the farm hand told me to stop so that the next batch of bales could be collected.

'Stop' he called, so I jammed by foot on the brake.

'Wheeey!' he yelled as he went flying towards the back of the trailer, nearly slipping on the carpet of straw and going head over heels to the ground. They decided I would be better on the ground from then on. Well, no one is perfect, are they?

We returned to the house after our hard day's work and John and I sat on the sofa, the strong aroma of hay still on our clothes. I really enjoyed being in a farming family in England and I was feeling a little sunburnt, tired and very contented.

'Let's go for a walk'. John suggested.

'We've only just got in. I'm a bit tired. I'm happy sitting on the sofa, resting. Let's stay here.'

'No, come on, we should go for a walk', John insisted.

I sighed. He really was a determined character. I guessed it wouldn't hurt me to go for a little walk.

Hand in hand, we walked up the narrow road. I prayed that no cars would come for I couldn't see how we could avoid being run over. We approached the gate to the next farm and stopped to admire the view. I peered in but none of their donkeys were in sight.

Suddenly John bent down.

'What are you doing?' I asked. 'Get up!'

Then I saw that he was on one knee like a hero in a Victorian novel. Was this really happening?

'I can only offer myself,' he started. I could hardly believe it. We'd only known each other for three weeks.

'Will you marry me?' The words were out.

I looked at this keen energetic young man and thought that life with him wouldn't be dull, no matter what happened.

'Mm.' I should've made him wait, gone home to think about it and taken my time in making such an important decision. But I didn't.

'Yes,' I said, thinking how life could be quite exciting and also how if I wanted a family, I should get on with it. Then I wondered if John knew what he was getting into, for as my brother says, I can be difficult at times.

Chapter sixty-nine

Our wedding

On the 23rd of February 1974 your granddad and I were married in the little village church at Paston Ridings near Peterborough. Dad came all the way over from Australia and gave me away. It was lovely, in a little village church in England where I'd always wanted to get married. My landlady's family kindly did all the flowers and the church looked beautiful. Even though February was in winter, on our wedding day, the sun shone as it has done on nearly every year on 23rd of February since.

We were both very nervous. All went fine during the service until it came to signing the register. On your granddad's turn to sign, he pressed the pen hard.

'Er,' he said, 'I've broken the pen!'

'Don't worry,' the vicar stepped forward. 'I think we can find you another.' He took the pen from John and disappeared into the vestry for a moment. He came back smiling, new pen in hand and the ceremony continued.

As we left the church as our friends showered us with confetti. I could hear the organist struggling with the Widor Toccata number five, a famous piece really meant to be played on a very big organ. When I'd asked the organist to play it, he'd said: 'On *this* little organ?'

'Yes, on this little organ.'

He grimaced, saying, 'I'll do what I can,' and still looking at me enquiringly hoping I would change my mind.

Our honeymoon was a whirlwind of new experiences and new places. We stayed overnight at the University Arms Hotel in Cambridge. This was exciting. We even had a TV in the room – quite something in those days. We flew to the Spanish island of Majorca for a lovely holiday.

I discovered that the famous composer Frederick Chopin had come to Majorca with his lover to stay in the warmth and try to get over an illness that was draining his strength. His old home was up in the lush green hills. I had to see it. Looking at the yellowing keys of his piano, I imagined him sitting there on a warm cloudless night, moonlight gently falling on the keys as his long fingers filled the cottage with the sounds of his lovely sad nocturnes.

We arrived back in England in the early hours of the morning. John started driving home. There were no other cars on the road until suddenly a police car pulled up and a policeman held up his hand asking us to stop. John pulled up and wound down his window.

The policeman stepped forward, shining his torch at our car. 'What are you doing?' he asked.

John grinned, a joyful newly married man. 'We're just coming back from our honeymoon,' he said proudly. 'Why?'

'Oh, it's just that it's a strange time to travel so we like to check.' The policeman glanced inside the car. 'I can see the confetti. Congratulations! You can go.' We were relieved. Tired and feeling very new and inexperienced, we returned our flat in Park Street in Peterborough. We settled back into work and began to establish a routine.

I'd always lived in a house that my parents owned. It seemed sensible. 'Renting a place,' I said to John, 'means that you are throwing your money away. If you buy a place, at least you won't lose all your money; you'll have the house to sell if you want.'

He looked into the cost of houses and how we could afford a mortgage and agreed that it would be a good idea.

'Well,' he said, bounding into the flat a few weeks later, with the same huge grin and the same joyful air that he had when I first saw him. 'I've done it!'

'You've done what?' I asked warily putting the teapot down on the table.

'I've agreed to buy a place in Sutton.'

'You have?' I held the pot in the air while I paused, trying to take it in. The tea splashed as I dumped the teapot down on the table to give him a hug.

'Wonderful!' Breaking free, I asked, 'Can I see it?'

John proudly drove me to Sutton and pulled up outside 2 Sutton Court. As I got out of the car, above the roofs of the houses opposite I could see the tower of the village church. It was solid and square, and I later learned it was called the pepper pot. We would be living in a real English village! I loved it.

The house had all that we needed: a garage, a sitting room, a kitchen, three bedrooms, a bathroom and a long stretch of garden out the back.

Chapter seventy

A piano

We soon settled in, but there was one thing missing: a piano. I asked a young teacher at the school, 'Do you know anyone who has a piano I can buy?'

'You can buy mine if you like.'

'Really! Don't you want it?'

'No, it's at my mum's house. I'll sell it to you for a tenner if you like.'

Wow, that was cheap, I thought and remembered to ask, 'Is it in good order?'

'Oh yes, Mum has had it tuned every year. Would you like to come and get it this weekend?'

'Sure!'

I then learned it was miles away, in Melton Mowbray. John didn't mind at all. Somehow, he managed to get hold of a van cheaply and brought the piano back from Melton Mowbray. The van stood outside our house, the doors open, the piano ready to be lifted out and pushed up the path and into the house. John looked at me and realised we needed more muscle power. It just so happened two men were walking past our house on the way home from the pub. We'd never met them before, but that didn't stop your granddad.

'Hey, you two!' he yelled. 'I've got a job for you.'

The men stopped and before they could move on, John said, 'Come on, come and help us get this piano inside.' A little taken aback, the men hesitated, shrugged their shoulders and then the three of them struggled the instrument into the house and next to the wall. John offered to pay the men, but they waved their hands; they didn't want anything. I had a piano! I started playing it straight away.

I loved the village. Most Saturdays I walked along the High Street to do the shopping. The longer we lived in the village, the longer it took, for I kept meeting people I knew and having long conversations.

One day I was talking to Sue Read.

'You know I've never really learnt how to sight-read music well.' I complained. 'Maybe we could get together and practise.'

'Yes, I'd like that.'

'Why don't you come around next Tuesday evening and we'll have a go.'

That was the start of a ladies' choir: first called 'The Warblers' and later 'The Isle Singers'. From then on, we practised every Tuesday at 2 Sutton Court. John loved to hear us sing and felt quite proud of his musical wife.

As time went by, the neighbours got fed up with listening to the choir singing lustily through their wall. They also began to dislike my piano playing which quite often consisted of scales and a lot of stopping and starting as I tried to improve my technique or arrange music for class. Soon, every time I struck the first notes, one of the neighbours started banging on the wall. It was then that I vowed that one day we would live in a detached house, like the one I had lived in in Tasmania.

We joined in a lot of the village activities. John was especially keen and joined the Feast committee. We dressed up as the famous gangsters Bonnie and Clyde and rode with Richard Swain in his vintage car that was just like the car the bandits used. It was great fun.

We also tried our hand at bell-ringing. A kindly chap, with a big round face and a body to match, patiently explained how I shouldn't let the rope to the bell go, because I could end up being hoisted right up to the bell mechanism at the top of the tower. Usually five of us took it in turns to ring our bells, sounding out different patterns. I loved the feel of the bell as it balanced just before I let it go and it rang out.

In the meantime, we were thrilled to discover I was pregnant. I felt a little sick at the beginning but otherwise I felt great. One day I went to Dr Jennifer Hughes, my doctor at the village surgery, for a check-up. She couldn't work out how the baby lay in my tummy. She asked another doctor to see what he thought.

Finally, she suggested, 'You may have twins', although she wasn't absolutely certain.

I went straight home. John was in the kitchen getting himself a coffee.

'How did it go?' he asked.

'Fine,' I said calmly, 'The doctor thinks we may have twins.'

He froze, went very pale and quickly stuttered, 'Y-you'd better sit down.'

I thought he looked as though he needed to sit down rather than me, but I sat down nevertheless.

'We have twins in the family, you know,' I offered. 'My grandfather was a twin. His sister was Aunty Wynn. I remember her when we were in Devonport. She used to give me a sixpenny piece every time we visited.'

I thought for a moment of all the sixpenny pieces I had collected from her and also found hidden inside Christmas puddings.

My tummy grew bigger and bigger with the possible twins. Eventually the doctor decided there was only one baby after all.

Chapter seventy-one

Our first baby

One night there was a concert in the church. John was busy, so I went on my own. There was very little seating, so I sat at the back, my heavy body making me feel uncomfortable, but I grinned, put up with it and prepared to enjoy the concert.

'Hello.' It was Eleanor Monk, the health visitor, who was also a member of my choir.

'I've brought my mother to the concert, but I have to leave early to go to a meeting, so would you mind seeing her home?'

I looked at my bulk and thought that maybe her mother should see me home as it was only five weeks before my baby was due. However, I agreed and walked this elderly mother to her home just round the corner from my house. I went home and crawled into bed feeling very tired.

At midnight, everything happened. I didn't know what to do. I still had five weeks to go. Then I remembered Eleanor and thought that she might be up late too.

'Things are happening. What should I do?'

'You should go to hospital in case.'

'Right.' I stood there holding the phone. 'John?'

The body in the other side of the bed didn't move. He stayed there, breathing deeply, obviously sound asleep.

'JOHN,' I shouted, pushing him. 'You've got to wake up. We need to get to hospital.'

'Mm?' He opened his eyes and when he realised what was happening, he shot out of bed and with trembling fingers, got dressed.

Once again, we were driving through Cambridgeshire in the early hours of the morning. The night was clear and the bushes lining the road were tinged with frost. There was hardly a car on the road, so the journey to Mill Road Hospital in Cambridge was quite swift.

Once in hospital it was all a blur. 'The baby is in distress,' said the doctor and immediately I was asked to sign a paper to allow them to put me to sleep and operate to get the baby out.

I woke up hours later, an operation scar really hurting but with a very worthwhile bundle of baby in my arms. This was our first baby, Jenny, a lovely little girl with red hair. She was so tiny she could fit between my wrist and my elbow. John was very proud and put up a sign on our window at 2 Sutton Court: 'It's a girl!'

We struggled to look after Jenny at first because we hadn't got anything ready for her.

In those days we didn't have any of the fancy modern gadgets for looking after babies. There were no disposable nappies at first, and even when they did appear, they were far too expensive. We had square terry nappies that we had to fold and put in a liner. We threw the liner away and soaked the nappies in 'Napisan' – that sterilised them. We had to put the bottles into a tank of water with a Milton pill to sterilise them.

I was still recovering from the operation and the baby needed attention nearly every hour day and night. Mum had died, and Dad and all my other relatives were on the other side of the world, so they couldn't help. John's Mum had enough troubles of her own, so we were on our own, which we said was what we wanted. However, I was getting really tired and one day I was SO tired that I put the baby into John's arms and said I was going out in the car to park somewhere and SLEEP.

I pulled the car into a lay-by, climbed into the back seat and lay down for a few moments of glorious sleep. Even before I had made myself comfortable and dozed off, there was a tap on the window.

'Oh no, what now,' I groaned and sleepily peered towards the window. There was the blurred face of a policeman. I slowly and with a great deal of effort wound the window down.

'What is happening?' he asked.

I slurred, 'I jussst wan some sleep' and slumped down on the seat ready to close my eyes again and have my well-earned doze.

'Can you tell me your name, please?'

'What?' I squinted at him.

After a long, mumbled talk with the policeman I finally convinced him I really did just want to sleep, and I was not trying to do anything worse. At last I was allowed that wonderful sleep that I had yearned for, for months.

John eventually agreed that we needed a detached house and we found a lovely one in Witchford. This is the house where I live now. It had a beautiful garden and four bedrooms, a perfect house for bringing up the children, for by now I was pregnant with my next child, your mum.

Chapter seventy-two

Witchford

On St Patrick's Day, 17th March 1978, when there was a little snow on the ground, we moved into our lovely house. It was like staying in a hotel that you owned. There was a wooden seat made of tree branches in the garden and every evening while Baby Jenny slept or played in the garden, I would sit there in the sun, admiring the pink and red roses that filled the garden and waiting for John to come home. He would sweep his white Ford Escort onto the drive and get out, looking so handsome. All was right with the world and I had a lovely capable man to look after me.

Then something happened that changed our lives forever. John had phoned me from a place called Oakham many miles away earlier in the day just before he went on an interview for a new job. He had sounded a bit distant, but I thought it was probably because of the phone line. In the afternoon, just after I'd put little Jenny down for a nap, I was about to have a little rest myself, when the phone rang again.

'Hello?' I was expecting it would be John again to tell me how he got on at his interview.

'Are you Mrs Westwell?' a young girl's voice asked.

'Pardon? Er yes, why?'

'It's Peterborough Hospital here. We have your husband. He was brought here by ambulance.'

I suddenly felt cold inside. My hands shook. 'Is he conscious?' I asked. The voice didn't answer. I said quickly, 'I'll come!' and slammed the phone down. What if I started having my baby early? There were only two weeks to go and I had to have an operation again, I had been told. What if the baby started while I was driving? What was I to do?

In shock, I rang the next-door neighbour to stay with me while I phoned around. We only had landline phones in those days, no mobile phones at all. I rang a kind friend and asked if he would drive me to the hospital. Then I rang Aunt Jean in Peterborough to ask her to go and see John. It would help him if he knew someone when he woke up.

When I got to the hospital, I found John in bed sleeping, a bump on his head and his eye badly bruised. Next to him was Aunt Jean. 'Hello,' she said giving me a hug. 'He came round and asked if you'd farrowed yet.'

I grinned. John was alright, even though he had had such a bump on his head. I didn't mind that he joked about me as if I were a pig, using the word 'farrow' for having a baby!

John stirred, came round again, grinned at me and was sick. He did this every half hour. To this day we don't know what really happened although it was suggested he had had an epileptic fit. John lost his sense of taste and some of his memory although gradually over time he regained these.

When I had my check-up about our second baby, I told the doctor what had happened. Immediately, I was whipped into hospital and your mum was born. This time I had very little pain but fearing that I would have the same trouble I had when our first baby was born, I asked for a few days to recover at the Grange in Ely where people could go to recover after serious operations.

I climbed into the taxi with our lovely newborn baby. As I looked at her, she pulled a face as if she was finding it difficult to breathe. Then I realised, the taxi driver had lit up a huge cigar and the fumes were filling the back of the car.

'Would you mind not smoking please?' I asked in my school-maamish voice. 'It is choking my baby.'

'Oh,' the driver said and reluctantly put out his cigar.

Your mum was gorgeous, had arrived at the right time, only wanted feeding every four hours and slept well at night. She was christened in her Dad's christening gown – a long flowing white garment. We called her Susan Claire. I chose the name 'Susan' and your granddad chose the name 'Claire'.

Your mum didn't cry a lot. She will be embarrassed now, but she used to lie naked on a blanket in front of our open fire happily kicking her legs to her heart's content.

Just before she was born, your granddad started showing signs of the illness that he now has. He tried hard to be the main person in the household, going out to work to keep his little family, but his illness prevented him. I realised if we wanted to stay in this lovely house and keep our family contented, I needed to go out to work full time.

Chapter seventy-three

Work again

One half-term holiday, I managed to get a job in a primary school and to find a childminder who would look after your mum and Jenny while I was at work. There was no playgroup in Witchford but your granddad worked hard to make sure a good one was set up.

The next five years were full of looking after two very lively little girls who, as soon as they could, argued. They were so different. Your granddad John, although he rode a bicycle to a factory to work, still needed me to help him, so I was very busy.

When Susie was very young she always looked neat and tidy, and she could have done with an organised and peaceful life. Our house was far from peaceful, for your granddad John was always interested in different schemes and different people, and I was always busy working, running the choir or doing the washing and ironing.

When she and Jenny had the chickenpox, Jenny had lots of spots all over her, but Susie only a few. They stayed in their pyjamas and dressing gowns, each with a bowl of camomile lotion to dab on their spots when they were itchy.

Every night, the girls had a bath before bed. It helped them quieten down and go to sleep. One evening, Susie was standing next to the bath dressed in a lovely blue dress, winter tights and shoes. Before I could do anything, she had stepped straight into the bath. I laughed. She stood there, the warm water seeping into her tights and shoes. When she realized she had forgotten to undress, she cried and cried. My laughing only made it worse for her, poor Susie.

We had a fair in Sutton and we all went. There was a competition to guess the name of a huge teddy bear. We all chose a name and Susie chose the name 'David' – the name of the boy at the child minder's. Lo and behold some hours later, Philip Read, a lovely Father Christmassy sort of man from Sutton and Susie's godfather, came knocking at our door. He was carrying a huge parcel – the teddy bear! Susie had won it. The bear was nearly the same size as her and she loved him. He was nearly always with her.

When Susie was about two, your granddad demonstrated his practical skills by building a special chair for her from some pieces of wood he had bought or acquired. He painted it white and added some colourful pictures of characters from the popular Children's TV programme *The Magic Roundabout*. Susie was VERY pleased.

After a very busy day, I would bathe the children, read them a story and put them to bed in their separate bedrooms so that they could get a good night's sleep. Every evening I would start to creep downstairs, but nearly every evening I would hear a little thump and the patter of little feet. Your mum was out of her bed and heading for Jenny's room. I went straight back up to the landing, put Susie in bed again and sat on the landing between the two bedrooms until both girls were asleep. We had no monitors we could listen to downstairs in those days.

Even when my dad, their granddad, came all the way from Australia to take us to a hotel at a beach for a good holiday, I still had to spend an hour or so in the evening sitting on the landing in the hotel to stop the girls disturbing each other when they should have been asleep.

Chapter seventy-four

Getting into mischief

We went to church in Sutton quite often and when we went to a service, Jenny was very inquisitive. She wanted to get out of the pew and explore, and I thought it better to let her go rather than struggle to keep her with me and have her squawk loudly. One Sunday to my horror, Jenny followed the minister as he was about to start the service and then stood next to him for some time. The newspaper reported how Jenny had 'helped' the service.

The girls were so lively that I found the best way to entertain them was to stay with them in the playroom in our new house in Witchford. One day I tried to take them to the hairdressers together. It was hopeless. One sat in the chair crying because she didn't want anyone to cut her hair, while the other careered around the salon trying to grab scissors or bottles of chemicals and peering rudely at strange ladies with weird headgear.

I decided that I would try to cut their hair myself. It couldn't be that difficult, could it? I would have both of them in the playroom and sit them one at a time on a stool in the middle of the room so that they couldn't grab anything. After all, I had crocheted a whole dress for baby Jenny. Unfortunately, she had immediately been sick on it and it never seemed to recover properly. I had sewn a whole dress out of the same green material for me and for Jenny when she was a little baby. I had also made some dungarees for the girls. I had a couple of university degrees already and was hoping to get more. I thought I knew it all.

Anyway, I bought a book on how to cut hair. That was all I needed. I followed the directions carefully, step by step, but when I looked, Susie's fringe was SO crooked. I tried again and again, but it just got worse. Realising she would have no fringe at all if I kept on going, I just had to leave it. No one had told me that the playgroup was going have the children's photographs taken. Oh, how embarrassing! Soon after that, I took them to a proper hairdresser.

At home, the girls loved playing in the front garden while I pulled out the weeds. One day, I'd pulled up some trailing plants with poisonous black berries on them and left them in a pile to collect after I'd cleared another part of the garden. When I went back, there was little redheaded Jenny giving little Susie one of the berries to eat. I panicked. She might be poisoned! I swept them up into the car and drove immediately to the RAF Hospital in Ely (now known as the 'Princess of Wales

Hospital'). I told the nurses what had happened. They said they'd keep the girls in overnight just to make sure they were alright.

When I arrived the next day to pick them up, the nurse looked very tired. She must have had a busy night, I thought.

'I'm so glad you've come,'

'Are the girls alright?' I was worried.

'Oh yes,' said the nurse, '*They* are perfectly fine. They hardly slept all night and we don't know how they managed to do it, but they broke one of our thermometers!'

Chapter seventy-five

Learning to read

It was nearly time for Susie to go to the big school with Jenny. This was the primary school in our village, The Rackham School, Witchford. Susie was a determined little girl, but if I suggested she did something, sometimes she would and other times she certainly wouldn't!

So, when I noticed she might be interested in learning to read at home, I put a pile of books I thought she might like on the bottom shelf of our bookcase.

'Oh,' I said in a distant sort of uninterested voice, 'these books are not for you, Susie. They would be far too difficult for *you* to read.'

Susie looked at the books and looked at me.

I crept out of the sitting room, so I could peek behind the door and watch what Susie was doing. Sure enough, she immediately grabbed one of the books, opened it and started trying to read it. When I wasn't looking, she would often creep into the sitting room and try to read the others.

Chapter seventy-six

Holidays

Dad always said that you need at least three weeks' holiday a year. One week to wind down, one week to enjoy the holiday and one week to wind up ready for work again. The doctor had told him this after Dad had been working too hard.

Granddad John and I both needed our breaks so we took holidays as often as we could. We went camping and we often went to a Butlin's camp where all the meals were provided and there were lots of things for the girls to do. We all loved it.

Then one visit to Butlin's was not quite as wonderful. Granddad John couldn't drive in case he had an epileptic fit, when he would go unconscious for a short time. He'd soon come round and be himself again, but he couldn't risk this happening while he was at the wheel. It was no problem for us in those days because I could drive us everywhere.

I was driving us to our usual holiday place at Butlin's in Skegness when Granddad John said, 'I feel sick.' Thinking he felt car sick, I said, 'Oh, just open the window; we can't stop now.' So he opened the window and I didn't dare look. It was lunch time so I pulled into a café. John said, 'I don't feel hungry.' He did look a bit 'green about the gills' as we used to say, so I suggested he lie down and have a rest in the sun while the girls and I went inside to eat. I put a handkerchief over the top of his head so that he didn't get sunstroke.

As we were enjoying our meal, someone rushed into the restaurant and yelled, 'There's someone outside having a fit!'

'Oh my gosh, John,' I said. We'd nearly forgotten him. We rushed outside and by now he was sleeping. I always took him to the doctor's after he'd had a fit, although they used to say you didn't need to. To my mind, he needed to see a doctor so that the medicine that he took to stop these fits could be changed.

I went back into the café and an ambulance was called and took John to the hospital. I drove there with the girls and saw that he was alright, nicely tucked up in bed overnight for observation.

As a result of this we arrived very late at the camp. We went to the restaurant and found almost it in darkness with only a few people there. I was hoping to explain that we needed help because John had been taken ill. No one seemed to be interested.

'Don't worry girls,' I whispered to Jenny and Susie, 'I'm about to throw a tantrum.'

Breathing in deeply, I yelled at the top of my voice 'WILL SOMEONE COME AND HELP US? WE'VE ARRIVED LATE BECAUSE MY HUSBAND HAS HAD TO GO TO HOSPITAL. YOU SAY YOU WILL HELP US WHEN WE ARRIVE, SO COME ON!'

The people in the restaurant froze. Eventually several of them rushed forward and we were given something to eat and shown to our chalet at last. John, still feeling a little fragile but otherwise fine, was able to join us the next day.

This was just one time when poor Jenny and Susie saw the side of life, when things didn't run as smoothly as we would have liked. I'm still very proud of how Jenny and your mum coped during their teenage years when their dad, Granddad John, gradually became worse, and eventually so bad that he had to be taken into hospital for always.

Before this happened, however, we had other holidays. Our friend Ken Featley let us borrow his caravan at a seaside place called Heacham. We had some lovely holidays in it.

Chapter seventy-seven

The storm

One day we were on the beach in our swimwear. The sky was cloudy but warm and we sat on our towels on the pebbles soaking in the sun or went for a paddle.

The tide was out so it was a long walk from the pebbles on the beach, across the damp sand to the first little waves coming in from the sea. Granddad John and your mum Susie were nearest to the water, I was just approaching them and Jenny was still on the pebbles. I looked at John and the sea, and I couldn't believe what I saw directly behind him.

There was a single huge black cloud. I'd never seen one so thick, black and menacing. It was so low that you could imagine touching it, although it was so full of danger, you wouldn't dare. It was very slowly following John, gradually getting closer and closer. Suddenly, a jagged lightning flash came straight from the centre of it down to the ground while a crash of thunder filled the air with angry rumbling.

'Quick,' I shouted. 'Run to the shore, there's a storm right behind you!'

Droplets of water fell on my face. The cloud crept even closer to John. He grabbed Susie and lifted her onto his shoulders ready to run.

'Don't do that!' I screamed, 'Susie will be the highest and will be struck first!'

He quickly lifted Susie down. By now hail was blasting us, cutting into our faces. I grabbed my towel, wrapped it round Susie and we rushed to the shore where we huddled together on the pebbles, waiting for the storm cloud to go away. Out of the corner of my eye I could see Granddad John hobbling slowly up the beach trying to reach us. He was soaked!

Fortunately, the hail eventually stopped and the storm went away. None of us were hurt and we were able to finish our holiday by the seaside without any more storms. But this incident alerted me to Granddad John's in-growing toenails and he had to go to hospital later to help him walk more easily.

Another day, the girls and I went to the beach while Grandad John stayed behind for a snooze. When we got back he woke up and got up from the settee.

'What's that mark?' I asked.

All over the settee was a big blue stain. John stared. He looked at his pocket and there it was – another huge blue stain. A pen had leaked! I dragged the settee cushion outside and frantically tried to get the stain off, but I couldn't. We had ruined it. We felt too ashamed to ask if we could use the caravan again.

Chapter seventy-eight

Birthday parties

From their first birthday, the girls had their own birthday party every year, Jenny's on or near the 9th of April and Susie's on or near the 6th September. We were poor in those days, so we always had the parties at home. Even though I was not an expert at cooking, I always made a cake in the shape of something that I hoped looked familiar, often a cat or a house, from the lumps of cake in the tins.

All their friends came. They sat around a big table and ate simple goodies like sandwiches, sausage rolls, jelly and, of course, cake. After lighting the candles on the cake, we sang 'Happy Birthday' and the birthday girl blew out the candles and made a wish. Then there were party games in the sitting room: Pass the Parcel, Musical Chairs, Statues and Sleeping Lions. In Sleeping Lions, everyone had to lie on the floor and stay absolutely still. If anyone moved, they were 'out'. After this I hid sweets in the garden and the children sped outside to find them. By then most of the parents had come and it was time to go home.

One memorable birthday, we used the ping pong table for our party feast. This was a large, heavy piece of wood balanced on a pair of A-shaped wooden frames. Just before we lit the candles, one of these supports collapsed and we watched in horror as all the party food slid slowly and unceremoniously down the table until the birthday cake fell with a plop into the birthday girl's lap.

There was silence. I laughed nervously and, thankfully, everyone joined in. We checked everyone was alright, rescued the cake and as much food as we could, put the table back together securely and started again.

As time went by, Granddad John came home from his factory job early in the afternoons, collected the girls from the school in our village and brought them home while I was still teaching at another school a long way away.

Fridays was special for them in those days. This was the day that their dad took them to Johnson's shop before bringing them home after school. They were given a tiny bit of money to choose sweets to put into little white paper bags the shopkeeper had given them. They were very careful to make sure they got a lot of sweets for the little money they had.

My choir The Warblers often gave concerts. One night I had to conduct a concert but couldn't get a babysitter so Susie came too. I told her to sit with some people in the audience. When I came to collect her after the concert, she was clutching a raffle prize . I hadn't given her any money for a ticket.

'How did you get that?' I asked.

'I won it at the raffle.'

'But I didn't give you any money to buy a raffle ticket.'

'These kind people gave me one.' Susie smiled at the strangers next to her.

'Well, you should have given them the prize!' I insisted.

'But Mum, I tried and tried. They told me to have it!' Poor Susie was quite pink with embarrassment by now. I shrugged my shoulders; this was one very lucky girl.

Later, when Susie was in the Senior School in the King's School, she told me afterwards about the time she was lucky to be alive. She went on a climbing trip and when the rest of the students had a lesson on how to stop if you found yourself falling down a cliff, poor Susie was ill and in bed. When she got better she went climbing again. Suddenly, she found herself falling. What was she to do? She had missed the lesson! To this day she doesn't know how she stopped herself, but fortunately for us, she was one very lucky girl once again and did manage to stop.

Chapter seventy-nine

A new school

Back at the Rackham School, they asked if they could move Susie up a class because your mum was very clever. I agreed, of course, and I think your mum was happy. She and Jenny went to ballet classes, and she showed a special talent. Unfortunately, the teacher moved away from Ely and it was too far for me to take them every week.

Then I saw an advertisement for a music teaching job at a private school in Ely. When I was brought up in Tasmania, everyone said that if you wanted a decent education you had to go to a private school. I'd always wanted my children to go to a mixed private school and when I discovered that the King's School in Ely was not only a good private school but had also started accepting girls, I applied a job there.

Nothing happened, so I telephoned the school, pretended I was someone important and invited myself to visit the school the next day to see what it was like. The Headmaster had answered the phone and was so surprised I had been cheeky, he agreed to show me round the school. While he was doing this, I explained how I wanted the music job and I could do anything he wanted.

'We're really looking for someone to teach rugby,' he said.

'I'm teaching rugby at my school at the moment,' I said. I didn't say I was only teaching rugby skills from a book when I took the classes for the physical education lessons. I was interviewed by three other important people, the main headmaster for the school said.

'We want someone who can play the piano very well. You must be able to play to a very high standard.'

'Oh, I got a scholarship.' I answered, not telling him that nearly everyone in Tasmania got a scholarship because there were so few people.

I got the job! This not only meant that I had a rise, but that both Jenny and Susie could be educated at the school for free. It also meant I had to play to piano often and in front of very important people, even Sir David Willcox, who had been the Queen's musician. I could never admit I was very scared and hated playing the piano in public. It was one of the challenges I had to overcome and you, too, will have many challenges that you will overcome to survive.

After Jenny started at the King's School, it was then Susie's turn. I thought they looked so different – Jenny was a redhead, Susie was blonde. Jenny looked like me,

Susie like her Dad, so I was amazed when the headmaster Mr Firkins looked at the junior children in assembly the first morning, glanced at Susie and said, 'Ah, there's another Westwell.' I think he was pleased.

One day when my class was lined up ready to go in, I glanced at Susie who was behind some boys. I was a little worried that gentle little Susie might not be able to manage the rough and tumble of the hardened boys at this private school. I heard a murmur from one of them and I saw Susie's foot push hard into the back of his legs. I decided that she might manage to survive after all.

I had warned Jenny and Susie that I wouldn't ask them any questions in case the other children thought I was favouring them. It must have been hard for them.

Every child who could sing was in the junior choir and your mum and Jenny both had lovely voices. One year when only Susie was in the school choir and it went down to London to the BBC to record, I had to choose a soloist. It was the one time I did favour Susie because she had the best voice in all the choir at the time.

One holiday we went by train to visit friends in Croydon. I wondered how to entertain the children, so I persuaded your mum and Jenny to sing all the songs they had learnt in the choir. When we came to our stop and were about to get out of the train, a lady came towards us.

'Uh, oh.' I thought we might have been too noisy for her.

'That was lovely!' she said. I was so relieved.

Chapter eighty

Australia

When your mum was about 11, I realised that if we didn't go soon to Australia, we would have to pay adult fares for all of us, which would be double what we had to pay at the moment. So the four of us, Granddad John, Susie, Jenny and I, went to Tasmania, . It was a wonderful trip and a chance for Susie and Jenny to meet my relatives. They loved my dad and got on well with my brother's two children, Stuart and Andrea. They didn't get on so well with my cousin Anne's children, Charles, Nick and Irving.

I like my cousin Anne and her husband Jim and in fact Anne and Jim and your granddad and I had got married on the same day –Granddad John and I in England, Anne and Jim in Tasmania. I was expecting Jenny and Susie to like their boys just as much. After we had visited for the day and the adults and children separated, I asked Jenny and Susie how they had got on.

'I hate them!' Jenny said.

'So do I,' said Susie.

I was so surprised. 'Why?' I asked.

'They locked us in a shed and wouldn't let us out.'

'Oh no.' I couldn't think of anything to say after that.

Jenny and Susie enjoyed many parts of their visit to Tasmania. They were able to touch and feed kangaroos, and see all the strange wildlife in the zoo including emus, wombats and fighting devils. They also threw pebbles into the Mersey River in Devonport where I used to live just as I did.

When we were in Devonport, I said, 'Come, I'll take you to the library so that you can join while you're here.'

We walked right to the end of town and to my horror the library was no longer there. I had been away from Devonport so long that they had moved the whole building to the opposite end of the town.

When your mum became a teenager, Granddad John had to go into hospital where he stayed for ever afterwards. In the house without him, it was very quiet and felt very empty. We missed him. We got a dog called Bramble who was fun and your mum used to dress her up, take photographs of her and take her for walks.

Your mum made lots of friends at the King's School and sometimes she would ask if she could spend the day playing with one of them. I came to realise that there were a lot of children of very wealthy people at that school. They lived a completely different life to ours.

One day Susie asked if she could play with a friend in the boats at the marina in Ely. When she said 'boats', I imagined little rowing boats.

'Who will be the adults looking after you?' I asked, worrying that they might drown if unsupervised.

'It'll be alright,' Susie said. I thought I would sort it out when we got there and, if necessary, would supervise myself.

When I drove her to the marina I realised why she was so certain everything would be alright. Of course her friends' parents would be there! They owned the whole marina!

Another time Susie asked if she could go to the cinema in Cambridge.

'Who will be the adults looking after you?' I asked.

'It'll be alright,' Susie said again.

This time I realised I needn't have worried because her friend had her own bodyguard who would go with them!

Chapter eighty-one

Teenagers

We all found teenagehood very hard, but we managed to get through it. Jenny was always too quiet, Susie had loads of friends but do you think either of them tidied their rooms? One day Susie's room was so bad that I took a photo of it declaring it a health risk. They were so lazy that after I'd ironed their blouses they let them fall into the dirty washing basket. That's why I still have a basket labelled CLEAN ONLY.

One day Susie was in bed and I could see she was very ill. She had a raging temperature. I said I was going to phone for the doctor to come. 'No, No!' Susie was adamant that the doctor was not to come into her room. She struggled to the car and I drove her to the doctor's for an emergency appointment. He told me to take her straight to hospital where she stayed for some days until she got a little better.

'When will you be able to come home?'

She scowled. 'They won't let me out until I eat properly.'

I tried to look sympathetic but inside I was cheering because I was always worried that the girls weren't eating properly.

I'd said to them, 'You are responsible for yourselves. You make your choices, but you have to live with them. If anything bad is going to happen, I'd rather it happened at home, but if there's anything illegal I'm reporting it to the police.'

We survived teenagehood reasonably unscathed, and while I'm sure they got into some scrapes that I may never know about, there was one notable occasion.

At the King's School, how the children behaved really mattered and reflected on the reputation of the school. Because I was a teacher there, I was expected to have very well-behaved children.

However, I drove into our drive one afternoon and as I opened my car door, I saw Susie sitting on her window sill, one arm over the side holding a cigarette and with a bottle of vodka on the window sill.

All I could do was shrug my shoulders and mutter to myself, 'That's my lovely teenage girl.'

Chapter eighty-two

At university

Jenny and Susie worked hard for their exams, did very well and both went to university. Susie went to university in Guildford to do a degree in languages. I always joke that she was good at languages because I used to talk to her a lot when she was a baby. They said if you did that, the baby would be very good at languages.

One time when she was a tiny baby being weighed on the scales by the nurse, I was prattling away to her, a baby who obviously could not reply, the nurse finally snapped, 'Any minute now she'll answer you!' We both knew that it was far too early for that to happen.

Part of Susie's course at Guildford University was to spend some time in Paris.

'Wonderful!' I thought and decided I had to go to Paris to see how she was getting on. We had a lovely time. Susie would choose a restaurant and I would pay, so we enjoyed a number of meals together.

In Paris, your mum looked just like a French girl going to work. On the metro one time, a couple of boys from Liverpool joined the carriage. They nudged each other, admiring how lovely Susie looked and, thinking Susie didn't understand English, started making crude comments about her.

'Cor, look at her, she's got … hasn't she?' one of them said. The other replied in a similarly crude way and I waited with bated breath while they kept this up for what seemed like a very long time. Susie waited too and finally snapped in her very posh private school voice, 'I'll have you know I am English!' I've never seen boys blush so much!

Chapter eighty-three

Being a nurse

It was very brave of your mum to decide that she wanted to be a nurse. Her sister Jenny had had a baby who had brain cancer and your mum supported Jenny a lot. That may have helped Susie make up her mind. She fought hard to get a place at Bournemouth University, worked at various jobs to earn enough money to keep herself and finally finished her degree in nursing. As you know, your mum now works as a nurse.

Afterword

Well, Harry, this has been a long tale of the 'olden days' before you were born, so I hope you've enjoyed it. Ask us some questions about it and I'm sure your mum or I can answer them. Perhaps, one day, you'll write a book called *Stories by Harry*. I look forward to reading it.

Love from Nanna Roe

Made in the USA
San Bernardino, CA
24 March 2018